*Dungarees*

## OPEN UNIVERSITY PRESS
### Gender and Education Series
Editors
### ROSEMARY DEEM
*Senior Lecturer in the School of Education at the
Open University*
### GABY WEINER
*Principal Lecturer in Education at
South Bank Polytechnic*

The series provides compact and clear accounts of relevant research and practice in the field of gender and education. It is aimed at trainee and practising teachers, and parents and others with an educational interest in ending gender inequality. All age-ranges will be included, and there will be an emphasis on ethnicity as well as gender. Series authors are all established educational practitioners or researchers.

## TITLES IN THE SERIES

**Boys Don't Cry**
Sue Askew and Carol Ross

**Untying the Apron Strings**
Naima Browne and Pauline France (eds)

**Changing Perspectives on Gender**
Helen Burchell and Val Millman (eds)

**Co-education Reconsidered**
Rosemary Deem (ed)

**Women Teachers**
Hilary de Lyon and Frances Widdowson Migniuolo (eds)

**Girls and Sexuality**
Lesley Holly (ed)

**Whatever Happens to Little Women?**
Christine Skelton (ed)

**Dolls and Dungarees**
Eva Tutchell (ed)

**Just a Bunch of Girls**
Gaby Weiner (ed)

**Women and Training**
Ann Wickham

# Dolls and Dungarees

## GENDER ISSUES IN THE PRIMARY SCHOOL CURRICULUM

### Edited by Eva Tutchell

Open University Press
Milton Keynes · Philadelphia

Open University Press
Celtic Court
22 Ballmoor
Buckingham MK18 1XW

and

1900 Frost Road, Suite 101
Bristol, PA 19007, USA

First Published 1990

*British Library Cataloguing in Publication Data*

Dolls and dungarees : gender issues in the primary
school curriculum. — (Gender and education)
   1. Great Britain. Primary schools. Curriculum. Sexism
   I. Tutchell, Eva   II. Series
   372

   ISBN 0 335 09287 X (paperback)

*Library of Congress Cataloging-in-Publication Data*

Dolls and dungarees : gender issues in the primary school curriculum /
   edited by Eva Tutchell.
      p.   cm. — (Gender and education series)
   Includes bibliographical references.
   ISBN 0-335-09287-X
      1. Sex discrimination in education — England.   2. Sexism in
   education — England.   3. Education, Elementary — England.
   I. Tutchell, Eva.   II. Series.
   LC212.83.G72E543      1990
   370.19'345 — dc20                                    89-39423
                                                            CIP

Typeset by Colset (Pte.) Limited
Printed and bound in Great Britain by Bookcraft (Bath) Limited

*To Judy and Suzy*
*and*
*Megan D'Arcy (born 2.2.88)*
*and*
*Sensible Footwear Theatre Company*

# Contents

Notes on Contributors                                     ix
Series Editor's Introduction                              xi
Acknowledgements                                         xiii
Introduction                                               1


SECTION 1:  WIDER IMPLICATIONS                             5

1   Contradictory Identities: Theory into Practice         7
    EVA TUTCHELL

2   What About the Teachers?                              14
    SUE WOOTTON FREEMAN


SECTION 2:  IN THE CLASSROOM: THE PRACTICAL
            IMPLICATIONS OF CHANGE                         21

3   The Use of Drama in an Anti-Sexist Classroom           23
    HELEN VICK

4   Design and Technology in the Primary Classroom:
    Equalizing Opportunities                               37
    BRIDGET EGAN

5   The Use of Construction Kits to Foster Equal
    Opportunity, CDT, and Collaborative Learning           46
    JO SHERWIN

6   Deepa's Story: Writing non-sexist stories for a
    Reception Class                                        52
    CHRISTINA SHAMARIS

# Contents

7   Mothers and Mother-Tongue Stories                                62
    LIZ FORSYTH

8   Tom, Dick and/or Harriet: Some Interventionist
    Strategies against Boys' Sexist Behaviour                        71
    ANNIE CAMPBELL AND NICOLA BROOKER

9   Towards a Non-Sexist Primary Classroom                           80
    SUE D'ARCY

10  Consultation, Persuasion, Adoption: Developing a
    School Policy on Gender                                          92
    DEREK TUTCHELL

11  A Joint Primary/Secondary Integrated Science scheme             100
    JOHN SIRAJ-BLATCHFORD AND JEREMY LOUD

References                                                          110

Index                                                               113

# Notes on Contributors

*Nicola Brooker* has taught in primary and secondary schools in London and now works for Berkshire's Language Inservice Curriculum Support. She recently took the Diploma in the Role of Language in Multi-cultural Education at London's Institute of Education.

*Annie Campbell* was born in Blackpool and has taught in primary schools in London, Slough and Windsor. Her main curricular interests are art, drama, PE and language development.

*Sue D'Arcy* is a primary school teacher, currently with a reception class in a Slough first school. She is a passionate advocate of equal opportunities for girls and boys.

*Bridget Egan* worked in primary schools in ILEA and Berkshire. A year's secondment researching CDT as a Teacher Fellow preceded her present appointment as Senior Lecturer in Design and Technology at King Alfred's College, Winchester. She has been active in the women's movement for a number of years and has taught women's studies courses for the WEA.

*Liz Forsyth* was a member of the Language Support Service in Berkshire for several years. She is now deputy head in a Slough first school.

*Jeremy Loud* After completing his training Jeremy taught in the tertiary sector in London. He has spent several years working in primary education, specializing in science and CDT curriculum development. He has also worked to promote and extend the use of computers across the curriculum. He is currently a classteacher and science co-ordinator at Foxborough Combined School, Langley.

*Christina Shamaris* teaches drama and English in Slough. For the past two years she has been a member of Berkshire Development Group for the SCDC 'Arts in schools' project. Her area of concern is to examine how the use of home languages could enhance learning in drama.

*Jo Sherwin* is originally from Canada, with diverse teaching experience in Italy and England. She is now head of Berkshire's Language Inservice Curriculum Support Team.

*John Siraj-Blatchford* is currently a teacher at a primary school in Waltham Forest. He had taught science for several years in secondary schools and had previously been in the electronics industry. His academic interests are rooted in the philosophy of science and technology and at present he is involved with curriculum development in the primary school and anti-racist science.

*Derek Tutchell* has worked in primary schools for over thirty years and is at present headteacher of Wykeham Primary School in Brent. He is and always has been an active member of the NUT.

*Eva Tutchell* is a feminist teacher who has spent many years working with others towards equal opportunities for girls and boys. She has taught in single-sex and mixed secondary schools in several LEAs and was recently seconded to promote gender equality in Berkshire schools. She is now also working in Dorset and at Southampton University.

*Helen Vick* is advisory teacher for primary drama in Berkshire. Although she has taught in all phases of education, much of her teaching life has been spent in middle schools run on primary lines. In addition to her advisory teacher role she has worked with B.Ed. students as a part-time teacher in drama in education at Bulmershe College. She believes strongly in the use of drama to challenge and reform attitudes to social issues.

*Sue Wootton Freeman* After several years teaching in primary schools, Sue is now Principal Lecturer in Education at Oxford Polytechnic where she is Field Chair of the B.Ed. for qualified teachers. She is also a member of the NUT National Advisory Committee for Equal Opportunities.

# Series Editor's Introduction

This book is a particularly welcome addition to the Gender and Education series since the primary sector has been somewhat under-represented in the volumes that have so far appeared. This comparative neglect of primary gender issues, however, owes more to the greater *visibility* of sex inequalities in the secondary sector, in say, option choices, examination results and career destinations, than to any prejudice on the part of the series editors. So, most of the pioneering work on anti-sexist practice was undertaken by secondary teachers and other educational personnel who had obvious wrongs to right.

It was more difficult to make the case for the existence of sexism in primary schooling though feminist teachers and researchers have made important contributions; for example, Katherine Clarricoates (1978), Carol Adams and Valerie Walkerdine (1986), Lesley Holly (1985), and the Anti-Sexist Working Party (1985). The philosophy of progressivism, child-centredness and the emphasis on the perceived 'happiness' of the child which emerged from the Plowden Report (1967) tended to mask social and sexual difference in primary school life.

It is only comparatively recently, with the publication of *Primary Matters* by the Inner London Education Authority in 1986, that anti-sexist primary practice emerged in its own right. However, the ILEA collection had only limited circulation and pre-dated consideration of the impact of the Educational Reform Act. *Dolls and Dungarees* is a worthy successor to the ILEA volume, and complements *Whatever Happens to Little Women?* recently published in this series. All three books take anti-sexist primary practice forward in the 1990s. *Dolls and Dungarees* offers *practical* guidance to those thinking of introducing an equal opportunities curriculum to their particular primary schools or classrooms for the first time. It further, and perhaps more importantly, indicates how anti-sexist initiatives can be sustained and expanded within the context of the National Curriculum.

It could be claimed that the concept of a curriculum which *all* primary children experience will render all equal opportunities work, whether concerned with race, gender or other forms of educational inequality, redundant. The authors of this collection, however, show that whilst a commonly experienced curriculum is promising, it is only through the recognition of the importance of successful primary anti-sexist strategies, that genuine progress towards a more just society can be achieved.

*Gaby Weiner*

# References

Adam, C. and Walkerdine, V. (1986) *Investigating Gender in Primary Schools*, ILEA.

Anti-Sexist Working Party (1985) 'Look Jane Look: Anti-sexist Initiatives in Primary Schools' in G. Weiner (ed.), *Just a Bunch of Girls*, Open University Press.

Central Advisory Council for Education (1967) *Children and their Primary Schools*, (The Plowden Report) HMSO.

Clarricoates, K. (1978) 'Dinosaurs in the Classroom – a Re-examination of some Aspects of the "Hidden" Curriculum in Primary Schools', *Women's Studies International Quarterly*, 1, pp. 353–64.

Holly, L. (1985) 'Mary, Jane and Virginia Woolf: Ten-year-old Girls Talking' in G. Weiner (ed.), *Just a Bunch of Girls*, Open University Press.

Inner London Education Authority (1986) *Primary Matters*, ILEA.

Skelton, C. (ed.) (1989) *Whatever Happens to Little Women?*, Open University Press.

# Acknowledgements

I would like to thank Barbara Humberstone, Margaret Littlewood, Jane Miller and Peter Ward for their help with this book. I am grateful for the patience and hard work of the contributors and also of Jane Beeson, who did far more than typing the chapters.

My thanks are also due to the head and staff of Godolphin First School in Slough, who have welcomed, encouraged and supported so many initiatives.

# Introduction

EVA TUTCHELL

This book considers the issue of gender equality in primary schools by focusing on some current classroom initiatives. It seemed to me that the aim of stressing good practice was most likely to be achieved if the majority of the contributors were teachers in direct contact with children and convinced that gender-related theories account for many differential power relations experienced in our primary schools.

In Britain we live and work in a patriarchal, capitalist system and, as MacDonald (1980) points out, 'one cannot disassociate the ideological forms of masculinity and femininity in their historial specificity from either the material basis of patriarchy nor [sic] from the class structure'. It is understandable that teachers may feel impotent in the face of such apparently overwhelmingly hostile odds. In schools we only see part of the problem and offer partial solutions. It is now 60 years since the battle for universal suffrage was won, and notions of gender inequality in schools are certainly not new (see Spender 1984) yet many teachers still feel either vulnerable or invisible in pressing for change. In the face of repeated rejection by those in authority at every level, teachers committed to gender equality do what idealistic teachers in adversity always have done: they find allies, make innovations in their classrooms and then collaborate to disseminate their practice through talk, research and published material. In gathering momentum and force, their ideas gain respectability and are generally addressed by a wider audience. It is a lengthy process.

Very few LEAs have appointed permanent equal opportunities advisers. Those that have, such as Brent and ILEA, have achieved change most rapidly (see Brent, 1985a, ILEA 1986). In Brent, however, excellent policies have suffered adverse publicity at the hands of a largely hostile national press. However, the implementation of new ideas needs careful and tactful handling, and there is no doubt that an insensitive and over-zealous attitude has led to unnecessary anxiety and even alienation among teachers in some LEAs.

At a different level, teachers are beginning to feel the pressure of the stunted philosophy of commerce in the form of a new vocabulary pervading our schools. We are being asked to 'deliver', to 'package', to 'market' and to 'audit'; the role of headteachers is being reduced to a form of managerial functioning, and teachers will soon be caught up in the cumbersome bureaucracy involved in monitoring the National Curriculum. No matter how efficiently schools are administered under local financial management, geographical location, employment prospects and living conditions will inevitably cause an even greater division than already exists in different parts of Britain and even within LEAs. The word 'teaching' has been replaced by 'delivery' and we talk of 'cohorts' and 'clients': whatever happened to *children*? The image being presented is of the deficient teacher lagging behind in a race being run in the marketplace. To exacerbate matters further, class sizes in many primary schools are growing, with some teachers now dealing with over 40 children with little (or no) classroom support.

It is against this divisive and fraught scenario that the initiatives in this book are being conducted.

Almost by accident, we found ourselves concentrating on the need for collaboration and consultation in addressing sexism in schools. In the words of Smith (1986): 'Teachers who want to introduce change even within their own classrooms, face an enormous force of inertia. It is difficult for one teacher, or even an entire school, to change in isolation.'

We are conscious of the danger of writing from an exclusive or 'White Eurocentric' (Amos and Parmar, 1984) position by concentrating on gender, but, as Lees (1986) has pointed out, 'all oppression takes place in a context'. I would argue that although questions of race and class are inextricably enmeshed with those of gender, their effects are often experienced in distinct and separate ways and the strategies for combating them are not necessarily the same. The schools we work in and write about here cover a diversity of populations and cultural groups.

Section 1 of the book concentrates on more general concerns: the changing context within which teachers work and the role of the advisory teacher supporting those who are challenging and combating stereotypical attitudes to girls and boys in schools. In Chapter 2, Sue Wootton Freeman considers the effects of the low status of women in primary schools and offers practical suggestions, based on successful courses in which she has been involved, to reverse this trend.

In Section 2 we visit actual schools and classrooms where anti-sexist strategies are being undertaken in a variety of situations. They are, perhaps, best regarded as separate case studies on aspects of the primary curriculum. Their purpose is to stimulate and encourage similar practice by teachers in other schools. The curriculum areas selected and presented here are in no way exhaustive, but they are all based on classroom experience which will be familiar to many teachers and relevant and accessible to other interested readers.

Drama is highlighted because children can readily absorb new concepts through role play and the other dramatic activities described by Helen Vick in Chapter 3. The value of craft, design and technology (CDT) in primary schools, particularly when used in a problem-solving context, is now being reappraised. It is obviously vital that girls are encouraged, from a very early age, to take an active interest in the manipulative and creative skills involved in CDT. In Chapter 4, Bridget Egan discusses the perception of CDT by young children and their teachers and how this can hamper equality of opportunity, while in Chapter 5, Jo Sherwin gives a detailed and entertaining account of anti-sexist measures that have been successful in boosting the confidence of girls in using construction kits in a first school.

Fiction exerts a powerful and constant influence in our lives. Stories and story-telling help to give shape to our daily experience. Children are fortunate in being able to slip in and out of fantasy with ease. It is therefore important that what Langer (1953) terms the 'virtual experience' they engage with through works of fiction helps foster a questioning and critical attitude to gender stereotyping. The list of good non-sexist fiction available is steadily growing and in Chapter 6 Christina Shamaris describes the host of interrelated issues that arise when her class of 15-year-old girls write non-sexist stories for the reception class in a neighbouring school.

In addressing bilingualism in Chapter 7, Liz Forsyth adds a new dimension to anti-sexist initiatives. Mothers of infant school children are usually welcomed into the classroom to help, but the kinds of task they perform often add to their low status image in the eyes of their children, particularly if they are black. The mothers described here, reading stories to young children in their mother tongue, not only gain in personal confidence as a result but also help teachers recognize the value of bilingualism in the classroom.

The intolerant and aggressive behaviour of the 10–11-year-old boys we meet in Chapter 8 and its effects on the girls in their class will be familiar to many teachers. The strategies used to deal with the problem can only be regarded as a temporary solution, as Annie Campbell and Nicola Brooker point out – ultimately a whole-school approach is vital.

In Chapter 9, Sue D'Arcy suggests practical methods to create a non-sexist reception classroom; in Chapter 10, Derek Tutchell takes us through the necessarily lengthy process of developing a whole-school anti-sexist policy. Finally, the successes and drawbacks of an inter-school anti-sexist and anti-racist science project are the subject of Chapter 11. The difficulties of matching secondary and primary schools' expectations and organization are explored and analysed by Jeremy Loud and John Siraj-Blatchford.

As an advisory teacher, I have worked alongside and learnt from the contributors to this book. All of us are committed to achieving greater equality of opportunity for children in schools though some of us privately take what Weiner (1986) would call an 'egalitarian' stance, and others adopt a more openly confrontational feminist approach.

We have chosen to write as accessibly as possible, including practical classroom details and also the humour that so often accompanies work with children. We have tried not to disguise the setbacks and constraints, but maintain the need to persevere in the face of opposition and apathy and also to share the infectious joy when strategies succeed. To return to Smith (1986): 'In collaborative enterprises, individuals help each other, and the enterprises become self-sustaining.'

Education, we know, is a process. This book is intended to give confidence and support to those engaged in change within that process. It is neither the beginning, nor should it be the end, of the story.

# Wider Implications

# CHAPTER 1

# Contradictory Identities: Theory into Practice

## The Role of an Advisory Teacher Seconded to Promote Gender Equality in a County LEA

### EVA TUTCHELL

*Several LEAs have appointed advisory teachers to promote awareness of gender issues in schools. Most are on secondment or have some kind of temporary contract. Their approach is thus inevitably somewhat cautious. Working alongside teachers committed to challenging stereotypes, a surprising amount can nevertheless be achieved.*

> I'd like to be a vet, but I expect I'll be a mother . . . EIGHT-YEAR-OLD GIRL (Holland, 1987)

> I do agree with most of what you say about equal opportunities, but no matter how hard you try, it will never change. It's always been the same. SIXTH-FORM GIRL

The first comment above encapsulates all too succinctly something of the overlapping problems facing the slowly growing number of teachers, myself among them, working in an advisory capacity to promote gender equality in schools by devising locally appropriate strategies. However, I feel sure that if, at age 18, I had felt as negative as the girl who made the second comment above (in response to a session on equal opportunities I had just run at her school in Berkshire) I'd probably never have bothered to get up in the morning. Although change is slow, and there are times when for every two steps forward we seem to take one step back, I am convinced that her pessimism is not justified.

The issues and attitudes surrounding the sexism experienced in our schools are many, varied and complex. There are no easy answers to the questions it generates. Nevertheless, on two points most teachers would agree: sexism is damaging to both sexes, and intervention is needed to trigger the necessary process of change.

Taylor (1985), a former LEA equal opportunities adviser, describes her experiences in implementing her LEA's equal opportunities initiative. A major contributing factor in her success was the open commitment of her LEA to gender equality.

The situation in my own LEA, as in most others, is very different. Although members of the Advisory Service are, and continue to be, sympathetic and supportive, any teacher taking part in anti-sexist initiatives is usually motivated by personal conviction and every school approaches the issues from different perspectives, based on differing needs and the individual experiences of *all* its staff. I am therefore surprised, but delighted, by the degree of active interest that I have found in a county LEA with diverse school populations and priorities.

My job description, negotiated with senior members of the Advisory Service, can be summed up as follows: to identify, encourage and promote good practice by evaluating initiatives in equal opportunities already undertaken, disseminating the ideas to other schools and raising awareness of central issues through inservice training.

I am conscious of the fact that although my LEA has a policy on multicultural education, the only official reference to gender equality is the meaningless statement in advertisements that the LEA is an 'equal opportunities employer'. However, since we live in a demonstrably sexist society, this has to be regarded as an expression of hope for the future rather than a description of present reality.

In a *Times Educational Supplement* survey conducted in 1987, 68 per cent of teachers questioned agreed that gender-based inequalities exist and need to be addressed. Yet, so many years after the suffragettes, Millicent Fawcett and Miss Buss and Miss Beale, and despite a growing wealth of literature providing evidence of gross inequalities, equal opportunities continues to be regarded by many as a 'sensitive subject'.

I have come to the conclusion that the reasons for this lie in the differential power relations experienced daily in our society and, furthermore, in the fact that sexism is not an issue we can safely leave in our workplace. It is present in our homes, where it can make us somewhat uncomfortable, because how we feel about our gender affects so many aspects of our lives. Most of us involved in education learn to live with our own prejudices and conflicts of interest in which our sexuality, our view of ourselves as parents or non-parents and as teachers with varying degrees of power play an important part. We respond to often unconsciously taken but fundamental decisions, allowing them to act as unspoken parameters, guiding our behaviour. This is how we 'make sense of the world' (Donaldson, 1978) and it gives us security, but can also limit and channel our thoughts and activities. When faced with the emotional risks implied in challenging this security, few of us respond with immediate unfettered enthusiasm. We tend to react with resentment, anger and even distress. None of these is easy to cope with and it is understandable that teachers, who feel undermined and undervalued at the best of times, will want to resist any such intrusion. But, whatever the initial personal discomfort, we cannot allow the blatant inequalities which exist to continue. What I have tried to develop are techniques for confronting the issues in ways which generate enough concern to activate teachers to respond confidently.

In a scene from one of my favourite films, *Singing in the Rain*, Donald O'Connor performs a virtuoso slapstick song-and-dance routine 'Make 'em laugh'. No matter how often I see it, it still *does* make me laugh. There are times when I realize that I appear to have adopted that song as my motto. Laughter often unites. 'Guilt-tripping' does not – it alienates and is divisive and is born of smug intolerance. It is wholly inappropriate in work where no attitudes remain permanently fixed.

## How change comes about for teachers

How do things get into people's heads? What makes it possible to accommodate new concepts? How are we persuaded not only to accept but also to act upon them? Those are the key questions with which I am constantly faced.

I have found, perhaps obviously, that new concepts are easier to assimilate if they can be made to fit previously held convictions, both professional and personal. If there is a clash of ideas then it is very likely that the less familiar concept will be rejected in favour of what James Britton (in Barnes, 1969) calls the 'nice warm dip together in comfortable beliefs'. Since teachers are the most effective agents of change in schools, they need support and they need to be properly resourced when taking the cold plunge into unfamiliar territory. I have therefore spent as much time as possible working alongside teachers in classrooms: team teaching, observing, taking small groups or individuals, teaching whole classes and being observed in turn, trying out new strategies and listening and talking, and constantly *learning*. This has allowed me both to rejoice in the successes and to share in the failures.

Because my brief is to cover the whole school age range, I can find myself in an A-level sociology class in the morning, followed by a drama lesson with ten-year-olds and ending the day reading stories with a reception class.

As a trained secondary school teacher, I am constantly aware of my possible lack of credibility in primary schools. My spectacular failure in a practical cookery demonstration with a group of six-year-olds, when in order simply to boil and fry eggs, every available utensil was used and the 'experiment' eaten before discussion of the results had begun, may have embarrassed me, but there is no doubt that it endeared me to the welfare assistant who rescued me and the teachers who, trying not to laugh, assured me that the children had *enjoyed* the 'lesson' enormously.

I spend time, deliberately, in staffrooms because they are an important part of teachers' lives and that is where I am able to take part in conversations about future plans and present frustrations. The important thing is to talk and think. In the words of one headteacher: 'I think it is very important for everyone to do their own thinking and to trust their own judgement. Most of all they should *keep on* thinking' (ILEA 1986).

It is through talking and thinking that we develop strategies, apply them, adapt them, start again. It is also through talk that we begin the vital process of networking.

## Networking

There are five teachers' centres in my LEA and all are extensively used by teachers. I have found that the networking (teachers co-operating and sharing ideas and resources on gender issues), begun through talk in individual schools, can be developed by teacher-led discussions, debates and demonstrations on teachers' centre courses. Not only do we thus alert and educate others, but the very act of persuasion builds our own confidence and sustains our energies.

We have held both 'twilight' sessions and whole-day conferences on many areas of the curriculum, including science, drama, pastoral care, reading schemes, teenage fiction, CDT, computer studies, constructional kits, single-sex schooling, race and gender issues, classroom management, collaborative teaching and learning, religions and cultures. Many of the teachers who come to these courses are enthusiastic about what they hear, and start to develop similar strategies at their own schools, and thus the cycle begins again.

### How change comes about for children

One of the themes running through the work of Walkerdine (1984) is that change does not happen passively but is a struggle to be actively engaged with. Having been a participant observer in a large number of lessons, I have witnessed the challenge of contradictory identities being met by individual children, both boys and girls, and by both teachers and children. Walkerdine (1981) looks at power relations between a woman teacher and two boys of nursery age. The boys, aged three, seem aware of the power of their offensive discourse. A little girl in the class is called a 'cunt' and the teacher is challenged to 'show off [her] "bum" and her "knickers" '. The teacher's progressive pedagogical style persuades her that these 'expressions are quite normal for this age'. Thus the boys' use of crude, sexual adult discourse displaces their teacher from a position of authority to a vulnerable, virtually powerless state. Less dramatically, I have seen children using every kind of strategy to negotiate power with one another, or more often to stake a claim for ascendancy in the classroom. It is a daily scenario, so familiar that it seems to go unremarked. 'Genderwatch' (Myers, 1987) has enabled some of us to pinpoint what is actually happening by focusing on specific details of behaviour.

Mary Willes (1981), in her study of discourse in nursery and reception classes comments on the fact that children 'know what is expected of them' at a very young age at school. My experience is that children also seem to 'know' that overtly sexist behaviour is likely to be frowned upon, but they have to feel safe to 'play' with anti-sexist ideas in order to assimilate them, just as we all do in order to learn.

This fragment of a conversation between myself and Asif, a bright six-year-old boy, wavering between a strongly defined sexist attitude and a striking ability to stand outside himself with humour, is evidence of one child's ability to come to terms with an uncertain identity. Asif, Minesh and I were looking at a photograph of a man holding a baby (Maidenhead Teachers' Centre, 1983):

*Asif*: That doesn't look right.
*ET*: Have you ever held a baby in your arms?
*Asif*: Yes.
*ET*: How did it make you feel?
*Asif*: It made me feel . . . 'laughy'. It was a nice smell.
*ET*: Was that talcum powder?
*Minesh*: Yes. My baby is two months old. We've got Postman Pat powder.
*Asif*: I've got He Man powder.
*ET*: Oh Asif, I didn't realise you were a He Man!
*Asif*: (*adopts a He Man posture*) Oh, Yes . . . (*collapses with self-deprecating laughter*) . . . Oh, NO!

On another occasion I observed Winston watching Avtar playing with dolls and a tea set. He seemed to want to be included but felt unable to ask. She was wary of inviting him to play, remembering several previous rebuffs. Half a dozen times Winston scattered her plates and dolls over the floor. Each time Avtar patiently picked them up without a word. Finally, she decided to let him into her world, but realized he might need to come 'in disguise'. She got up, found a hat for him to wear and said, 'Come and help with our picnic party'. He joined her with alacrity, aided by the role play implied by the hat.

There are many examples of girls' achievements in other chapters in this book, so I shall restrict myself to one example where a change in my own attitudes facilitated a similar change in a seven-year-old girl. In September, Louise said firmly 'I can't!' when I offered her various construction kits to use. I tried to encourage and persuade her, but she remained reluctant and moved towards the safety of the jigsaw puzzles, in the corner of the room. I realized that my own unfamiliarity and lack of facility with construction kits was contributing to her rejection of the activity. Over the next months I overcame my own inhibitions and started to enjoy 'playing'. Gradually, Louise joined me for longer and longer periods, becoming absorbed and competent. In May I observed her holding her ground in the middle of the floor space provided for this work, refusing to be elbowed out by the boys to the fringes where previously she had been content to stay.

I have long been convinced of the need to develop anti-sexist strategies with boys as well as girls. Despite the undoubted and completely unjustifiable greater power wielded by men in our society (and therefore perceived even by the youngest boys as an indicator for their future roles) no one is *born* an oppressor and I am reluctant to lay the blame for patriarchal attitudes totally with conspiracy theories. The reality is far more complicated. Masculinity and femininity are constantly being constructed and reconstructed by all of us. I leave the last words with Stephen, aged eight and outwardly very aware and protective of his masculinity. He is writing a caption for a photograph of a (male) ballet dancer, rehearsing, wrapped in an assortment of woollen garments (Brent, 1985b):

> I am a dancer
> I lik it
> I wood lik to aper on TV
> I haf to be fit
> And I haf to hav
> Fik clos.

# CHAPTER 2

# What About the Teachers?

## SUE WOOTTON FREEMAN

*There are far more women than men working in the primary sector of education, but this is not reflected in their prospects for promotion. Low status can produce low self-esteem. Sue Wootton Freeman suggests ways in which specially devised courses can raise the confidence of women teachers in applying for promotion and in interview situations.*

As we attempt to enable the children in our schools to form a more complete picture of their abilities and worth by encouraging non-stereotypical behaviour and choices in respect of materials and experiences, we must ensure that the staffing structure of schools reinforces rather than undermines our work. Experience of adults demonstrating a variety of roles is a valuable tool to encourage children in exploring possible roles for themselves and in the formation of accurate estimations of life chances. Peter Kahn, a nursery teacher writing in *An Equal Start* for the EOC (n.d. (a), p. 30) draws our attention to the need for men to work with young children:

> The models that adult men present to young boys and girls are firstly incomplete, and secondly remote. Incomplete because not many men feel able to show the caring and nurturative side of their personalities, feel able to be gentle and to show their feelings. Remote because – with few exceptions – men just aren't around, caring for, teaching and playing with young children.

Further, in a publication on the underrepresentation of women in senior posts in schools, the EOC (1985, p. 4) notes 'a lack of models of women in positions of responsibility which could have an adverse impact on the aspirations of girl pupils'. If all children are to see that caring, sensitive and authoritative, powerful roles are appropriate to men and women alike, then they should be able to observe and experience this in their schools.

The fact that about 70 per cent of primary school teachers are women does little to raise the status of the job. Its association with the 'caring' side of child-rearing and the relatively poor prospects for promotion do not attract large numbers of male teachers. Primary schools now receive proportionately few incentive allowances, and few have had promoted posts at, or above, scale 3. Secondary schools, being larger and attracting more revenue per pupil, have had more developed structures in terms of posts of responsibility and opportunities to experience middle-management roles. However, primary schools, by virtue of their number, have at least been able to offer the attraction of very many more deputy head and headship posts than their secondary counterparts, although a disproportionate amount of these still go to men.

It would seem reasonable to expect that, given the large number of women teachers in this sector, the proportion of women achieving promotion to deputy head and headship would be substantial, roughly in line with their total presence. In this area the children would then have the opportunity to gain an understanding of the possibilities for women as managers and authority figures. However, the proportions of women achieving deputy and headship posts bear no relationship to their representation in the teaching force. Approximately 37,000 men teach in the 25,000 schools in the primary sector. In 1985, 7 per cent of women in primary schools were heads and 8 per cent deputies, while 32 per cent of men in primary schools were heads and 20 per cent deputies (NUT, 1987). Conversely, 77 per cent of women teachers in this sector were on scales 1 or 2 (main professional grade) compared with only 36 per cent of male teachers.

The NUT/EOC research project 'Promotion and the Woman Teacher' in 1980 made it crystal clear that many of the traditional 'explanations' for this phenomenon were simply not founded. The assumption that women teachers 'are all middle-aged married women preoccupied with family commitments' (EOC, 1980, p. 51) could no longer be valid. Over 80 per cent of those polled in their survey described themselves as actively pursuing a career, giving the lie to the myth that women are not interested in teaching careers. Fifty-one per cent of the sample had applied for promotion within the previous five years and 77 per cent saw themselves as teaching until retirement. Only a third of the research sample had children of school age and a third of the women teachers were unmarried.

It is clear that the career break which is taken by some women teachers to produce and raise their families does irreparable damage to their career prospects. The time when experienced teachers begin to move towards posts of increasing responsibility en route to headship seems to correspond roughly with the point at which child-rearing may preoccupy many women teachers. Despite the length of service still to come for many women returners, often in excess of 20 years, their prospects of promotion are slim. Indeed, they often experience great difficulty re-entering the profession at all and have to take part-time or supply work as a first step back. Although this may suit some teachers as a bridge between full-time child care and full-time teaching, it is the only re-entry route for many and means that they return to their careers with very reduced status and pay.

It appears, however, that the mere prospect of a break in service, rather than its reality, affects the likelihood of promotion of many teachers, even those to whom it may not apply. The incidence of irrelevant questioning at interview is high, centring around the family life of women teachers, and betrays the assumptions of biased interviewers. 'Do you intend to get married in the near future?' (West Kent NUT, 1985, p. 6), 'Who will care for the children if they are ill?' (EOC, 1980, p. 38), and 'Do you intend to have more children?' (West Kent, NUT, 1985, p. 6), are all examples of questions which contravene the recommendations of the EOC (1985, p. 10) that

> Questions at interview should not be different for male and female candidates. Questions about marriage plans or family intentions or childcare arrangements should not be asked, as they could be construed as showing bias against women. Applicants' sex, marital status, children and domestic obligations should play no part in the selection process.

Thus the assessment of professional competence for a post is frequently clouded by stereotyped views of a woman's ability to perform in the workplace which are largely bound up with her child-rearing potential and the subordinate nature of her career to that of an assumed partner. In Clwyd, a question was even asked about the date of female interviewers' last period.

It is doubtful whether many women were ever really able to work as teachers for 'pin money' (the main wage supposedly being earned by the husband) although during the 1970s there was some belief that this was the case. Certainly, I have never met such a teacher in 16 years of professional life and it is now quite clear, with changing patterns of work and family life and highly developed lifestyle expectations, that few women could fall into this category. Economic necessity and/or the desire to work full-time at a professional career have long since become the driving force for most women teachers. Also, women are less likely to be encouraged to go on management training courses.

Few education authorities keep the kinds of statistics which would enable researchers to ascertain the numbers of women applying for promoted posts, particularly heads and deputies, but there seems to be not only a general drop in headship applications in some areas of Britain, but also a specific decline in the number of women applicants. One may speculate that factors in women's perceptions of the job may deter application, such as the management style adopted by male heads of the 'benevolent despot' type. Women, on the whole, seem to prefer a consensus model of management (see Wallis, 1987, pp. 80–2) which may be at odds with the role models previously encountered. Where a co-operative model of management, based on group decision-making, is in evidence, it seems to work well and to be particularly suited to the situation in primary schools. It may also seem to many women, especially in schools which, because they are small, have a head who also teaches a class full-time, that the quality of life both in and out of the workplace will be adversely affected by the enormous pressure of this dual role. There are few arguments to counter this view.

During the last decade, clear attempts have been made by teacher unions, especially the NUT, to improve the career prospects of women teachers. From the NUT/EOC survey onwards, there have been increasing numbers of courses directed towards enabling women to develop their own professional careers and personal potential. Many women have become involved at national and local level in fact-finding, negotiating and initiating further training. Supportive material from the EOC (n.d. (b);

1980) has become available and brought increased understanding to those who have grasped its importance. Some authorities, such as Kent, have begun to see the potential benefits of shouldering their responsibilities towards their employees and have implemented a scheme of career development for women teachers which includes a returner scheme, a job-sharing scheme, career development counselling for all staff and in-service training courses on 'Career Development for Women Teachers'. But the hierarchy is still excessively male.

However, some women in primary schools at the time of writing are reported to be leaving unions which took extended action in support of the pay dispute (particularly the NUT and NAS/UWT). The desire for consensus models in schools mentioned earlier may well have made the last few years almost intolerable and removed the quality of professional life so far from the ideal that some women felt that they had no alternative but to transfer their allegiance. Certainly the size of an average primary school and the closeness of the relationships with parents and children make it possible for a teacher taking action of a conventional nature to feel very isolated and acutely aware of the damage inflicted on children and parents in this way. It was a measure of the desperation of such teachers that they were ever able to take action at all. However, a number of women teachers also became very politicized and took important roles in local disputes.

The near future brings a mixture of measures in terms of women's careers. While some education authorities, such as Kent, have instigated measures designed to make governors and others involved in the recruitment of teachers aware of the inappropriate expectations that they may bring to the interviewing procedure, and to implement measures designed to promote women teachers' career development, the proposals currently going through Parliament to allow schools to opt out of local authority control will mean that in the future such schools need take no account of the authority's policies. Further, school governors will have the right to hire and fire teachers and, judging by the improper questions still asked at interviews, many factors other than professional competence will be considered. The Teachers' Pay and Conditions Act 1987 ensures that teachers employed under its provisions, returning after a break in service, do so to at least the same point on the salary scale as they left, though years of raising children no longer count towards incremental points. This is an improvement upon the previous position where it was not only possible but highly likely that a teacher who had taken a break in her career, having achieved, perhaps, deputy head status, would be most likely to return at main professional grade, albeit with some incremental allowance for her unpaid experience. However, the same Act also allows education authorities to determine a rate of pay for supply teachers – of whom a very high proportion, probably over 90 per cent, are women – regardless of their years of experience and level of expertise. The devolution of financial management to the largest primary schools brings further pressure to bear upon their headteachers which will increasingly cause potential applicants to consider their quality of life within and outside the school.

None the less, it is clear that, if children in schools are to be given the chance to benefit from adults demonstrating a variety of non-stereotyped roles, continuing pressure has to be brought upon teachers' employers to ensure that proper account is taken of measures to improve women teachers' promotion prospects.

In 1985 the National Advisory Committee for Equal Opportunities was established by the NUT. Members are elected from regional divisions of the NUT for a three-year period, and meetings are held once a term, though working parties set up by the National Advisory Committee meet far more often. One outcome has been the publication of a pack, *Towards Equality for Girls and Boys* (NUT, 1988), concentrating on children and the school curriculum.

A great deal of time, however, has been devoted by members of the National Advisory Committee to developing the careers of women teachers. Members have been able to exchange valuable ideas and information on courses that several local NUT associations have run, specifically to encourage women to apply for promotion.

Most have been one-day courses, either on a weekday where supply cover has been made available, or, more often, on a Saturday. All have been extremely well attended, some oversubscribed, and they have generated enthusiasm and pleas for more. Many women teachers, as a consequence of such sessions, have decided to participate in assertiveness training courses. The following, organized by the Oxfordshire division of the NUT, is typical of the kind of programme offered:

WOMEN'S CAREER DEVELOPMENT

Thursday April 2nd, 1987, Guildhall Abingdon.

PROGRAMME

|       |                                                                          |
|-------|--------------------------------------------------------------------------|
| 9.30  | Coffee and Icebreaker Exercise                                           |
| 10.00 | Brief introductory talk by Sue Wootton Freeman                           |
| 10.15 | Career/Life Planning Exercises                                           |
| 12.00 | Lunch                                                                    |
| 1.00  | Talk by Bev Anderson of Oxford Polytechnic – 'Getting as far as the Interview' |
| 2.00  | Interviews – introduction and brief discussion                          |
| 2.20  | Interview practice groups                                                |
| 3.40  | Plenary session of feedback from groups and evaluation.                 |
| 4.00  | Close                                                                    |

By far the largest part of the day is taken up with workshop activities designed to enhance the participants' confidence and skills, with ample reading material and further exercises to be used in their own time. The teachers are very enthusiastic about the work which they do and evaluation sheets show a good spread of support for the various activities, but only time will tell how far their chances of success are enhanced by such courses.

There is a great sense of frustration at the obstacles to women's career progression, and internal promotions are a source of dissatisfaction still, despite the union's guidelines, and the issue of age in relation to career progression is referred to repeatedly.

There is overwhelming support for further courses, both of this kind and by way of follow-up to such initial exercises. A large proportion of the participants feel that courses need to be longer and, although there tends to be clear preference for day courses with supply cover, given certain variables such as crèche facilities, many feel that weekend courses should be run. (See also the excellent training pack published by Bradford Metropolitan Council (Bradford, 1986).)

It can only be to the advantage of teachers' employers to ensure that they utilize the talent, experience and expertise of all their teachers. Underuse of women teachers' potential is wasteful and frustration is destructive. The law demands that there should be equality of opportunity for all teachers and proper attention to this area would bring a long-awaited boost to women teachers' morale.

# In the Classroom: The Practical Implications of Change

# CHAPTER 3

# *The Use of Drama in an Anti-Sexist Classroom*

## HELEN VICK

*Drama in schools is in danger of being marginalized by the National Curriculum. Using examples of her work with groups of primary school children, Helen Vick demonstrates the value of drama in developing and fostering awareness of gender issues in imaginative and non-threatening ways.*

The following exchange was part of a drama lesson with 30 nine- and ten-year-olds in a multi-racial classroom. I was taking part, as teacher-in-role, with the express purpose of challenging the group's assumptions about gender roles.

> *Alien* (teacher-in-role): Come in starship. Are you receiving me?
> (*Initial confusion among the children who are involved in the drama*)
> *Commander* (a girl): We are receiving you.
> *Alien*: You are being held in orbit round our planet. Please identify your leader.
> *Commander*: I am the Commander.
> *Alien*: Are you male or female?
> *Commander*: Female.
> *Alien*: Good.
> (*The alien asks for the navigators, who are female, to be identified, and expresses approval*)
> *Alien*: Please identify your engineers.
> *Commander*: Gurdeep and Shaun.
> *Alien*: Are they male or female?
> *Commander*: Male.
> *Alien*: Impossible! Repeat. Please identify your engineers.
> (*Confusion among the crew, who gather round the commander to give advice*)

*Commander*: (*lying*) Female.
*Alien*: We have detectors which will check the accuracy of your
   answers.
(*Other members of the crew are identified until the alien asks
about the explorers, who are boys. This time the Commander
makes a stand*)
*Commander*: They are male.
*Alien*: Repeat. Are your explorers male or female?
*Commander*: (with careful emphasis) OUR EXPLORERS ARE
   MALE.

In drama I work from the basis that children are protected by
their roles because drama is like a game. Pupils may be fully
absorbed during the make-believe, but the consequences of their
actions and decisions do not carry on directly into real life.
They can stop the drama, but if it has been a meaningful experience, they carry what they have learned from it into their real
world.

One of the first problems a teacher tackling any assumptions
about gender through drama may have to face is the self-
segregation of boys and girls. The ways I have found to deal with
this depend on the children, the circumstances and what my aims
are for the session. At times it is most appropriate for children to
work in friendship groups, which are usually single-sex groups.
Often children will see the need to work in mixed groups where
this best suits the context of the drama, for example when the
children are being villagers grouped into families.

The non-sexist teacher might see the dilemma working with
mixed groups when the subject matter is historical and/or domestic. On the one hand, she/he is pleased that the boys and girls are
happy working together; on the other, she/he recognizes that the
girls may be relegated to second place by the traditional female
roles they are allotted.

In my work as an advisory teacher where I often only work
with a group on a few occasions, I sometimes impose a gender
mix on the children. At other times I group them, using mixing
games and devices to make the groupings arbitrary.

I propose, in this chapter, first to describe a lesson where I used
small-group improvisation to address gender issues, and to offer
hypotheses about the way that drama, as a valuable teaching
tool, can affect children's attitudes. Then I will discuss the space
lesson quoted above, and I will end by describing a piece of

theatre I worked on with children in which we explored a real issue that had cropped up between girls and boys in their school.

## Lesson 1: Exploring assumptions related to gender

Imposing mixed groups, I devised a lesson with fourth-year juniors specifically to tackle gender as an issue. The teacher, a man, had read *The Turbulent Term of Tyke Tiler* (Kemp, 1979) to the class but otherwise not much work on gender had been undertaken. This was to be a simple small-group drama session interspersed with whole-group discussion. My aim was to raise the children's awareness of the assumptions they make about gender roles and also to experiment with reversing gender roles in an attempt to widen their perceptions.

After a 'warm-up' in mixed pairs, I gave a mixture of written and verbal instructions. The written instructions were as follows:

> You are members of a household containing two adults and two children. It is tea time. One person is making the tea. One child has got good marks for a science project. One child has just played a match with the school team. One adult has just been offered a promotion at work which would involve a move to a town 100 miles away.

And the verbal instructions:

> Discuss around the tea table whether the household should move so that the adult can take up the promotion. Such a move would affect each one of you, so make sure you have a chance to give your views.

The groups were left to allot roles as they chose and start their improvisation.

After 10–15 minutes I stopped the role play, and, through a quick show of hands, took a survey of how roles had been allocated and also enquired of the groups, who had done most of the decision-making during allocation. It was also interesting to hear whether, from the improvisation so far, the members of the household were intending to move or stay put.

The results showed a clear polarization of gender roles. In all seven groups a boy had been chosen to play the adult (usually father) who was offered promotion. In every case it was either the mother or the daughter who made the tea. I was surprised by this strict gender division in this nearly all-white middle-class area, where some of their mothers must have had professions. The choice of child roles were fairly equally represented; some girls got high marks for their science projects, some played for the netball team. (Attempting this session again I would perhaps suggest that one of the children has just seen the careers officer. The choices of career could be revealing.)

It was interesting that, on being asked, the boys and girls claimed equal responsibility for role allocation. In the improvisations most families tended towards moving house to follow the man's career. I then asked the children to reverse the functions within the roles, so that 'mother' was to be offered promotion, 'father' or 'son' was to make the tea. They did a further improvisation, not bound by what had happened in their first version.

In discussion afterwards I asked the children to reflect on their experiences in these new roles. I found the boys to be more amenable to change than the girls. One lad said: 'I liked being in the kitchen, it was peaceful there.' Two girls said that it did not feel right being the main breadwinner in the family. Using my survey of their initial role choices as a vehicle, we had a general discussion about gender roles. Though the class freely admitted that boys and girls achieved equally in school (one boy actually admitted that 'the girls are brainier in our class') the boys still argued that men should be the main wage earners. The boys grew quite heated as a result of my challenges and supported one another loyally. In the end, they put male superiority down to physical strength. There were certain jobs such as building that women could not do, they claimed. The girls had little to say for themselves and were disappointingly quiet. We were stopped by the bell and the teacher asked the class to line up, girls on one side of the door and boys on the other, a touch of irony I could not resist commenting upon.

I tried this lesson with another group of children who had been examining gender roles as part of their curriculum. They were less conventional in their allocation of roles. At least one girl played a mother who had been offered promotion and in another group one boy chose to be mother.

In discussion, which we conducted in three groups (one adult in each), I was pleased that the girls were much more confident in defending their right to equality than in the first group I worked with. However, now that the children were speaking for themselves, unprotected by a role, polarization between boys and girls again occurred, the boys again using physical strength as a reason for superiority.

### Does the teacher affect children's perceptions of gender roles?

Where does this polarization between boys and girls start? It is tempting to blame the home and the media, but the influence that teachers have on children should not be underestimated. I find myself asking whether, in choosing traditional fairy tales and nursery rhymes and ring games, infant teachers are actively enhancing gender and other stereotypes and also exacerbating the problem by introducing all-good or all-bad characters. I have heard the argument that children need one-dimensional characters to symbolize and externalize their own positive and negative feelings. (I remain sceptical.)

Walkerdine (1984) describes her research into pre-teen girls' magazines. She finds that the stories invariably seem to parallel traditional fairy tales. Heroines, the 'good' characters, are generally depicted as innocent, passive victims who win the day by being long-suffering, selfless and pure, while characteristics such as aggression, self-centredness and jealousy are attributed to separate 'bad' female characters. No suggestion is made that both types of characteristic could be contained within the same personality. If fairy tales contribute to a division in the female psyche at an early age, it is not surprising that women often feel 'all wrong' about being assertive.

Simple elimination of such fairy tales from the 'diet' of young girls would not seem to be an easy solution. Walkerdine insists that the stories have a powerful emotional appeal, dealing as they do with relationships on the level of fantasy. She points out that teaching about gender which presents facts and logical argument without engaging the emotions is unlikely to alter fundamental attitudes. What is needed is an alternative form of fiction.

Drama is surely such an alternative. Drama is a medium through which children can simultaneously create a shared fantasy and actively participate in it. Inherent in drama are the dynamics of relationship: conflicts to be worked at, tensions to be resolved. Walkerdine suggests that femininity and masculinity should be explored, 'not as fixed or appropriated, but struggled over in a complex relational dynamic'.

When working at school I find that young children move easily in the world of fantasy, so I use fantasy situations to challenge the stereotype gently. The dragon may be a coward, the monster well-intentioned but misguided, the all-powerful king asks for the advice of the villagers. One multi-ethnic group of five-year-olds, on helping me construct a giant which was to be our central character in a drama, decided that she was a lady giant. Furthermore, they instructed me to draw her with a brown face and she was to be smiling. I felt this class, on being given the choice to break the stereotype, had gained real 'ownership' of this character even before the drama started.

In attempting to avoid stereotypes in my work in infant schools, I often feel I am working against the scrupulous laying down of a static culture base. Children's concepts are only just forming and I am aware of how vulnerable they are to being confused by different cultural messages. I feel a pressure (not necessarily external) to conform to cultural norms to avoid confusing the children. Yet, I have to remember that these are the citizens of the future and that I am committed to working towards a more equal society.

I am convinced that if these children receive their concepts of fixed gender roles because no one wants to disturb the status quo and confuse them, work in gender equality when they are older may only ever touch the surface. It may be possible, later, to appeal to objective reason and sense of fairness, while leaving deeper, 'gut-level' attitudes intact. How many of us, considering ourselves reasonably enlightened, from time to time experience unwelcome and puzzling 'gut' reactions deriving at an early age from the influence of parents and others who did not believe in equality between genders, races and classes?

Drama is closely related to children's imaginative play in that it offers a safe framework of 'pretend' for anything they want to explore. The difference between free imaginative play and drama, in my opinion, is the structural intervention by the teacher.

Left to their own devices, children can be very inventive, but they can also fall into the rut of mimicking or rehearsing stereotypical behaviour picked up from those around them and from the media.

The teacher, by careful structuring and negotiating with the children over selection of roles and contexts, can widen children's experiences and fantasies within the drama, whether simulated or based on fantasy. The teacher can deepen their perceptions by using strategies that address the issues underlying the children's action-packed story lines. A useful technique is that of teacher-in-role, where the teacher takes a role in the drama. This technique enables her/him to organize and control in a non-overt way; to introduce and elicit ideas and information; to empower the children by treating them as experts; and to demonstrate her/his own commitment and belief in the drama which has the effect of encouraging theirs. The possibilities are considerable. By interacting with the children in the drama she/he has access to the learning potential within the children's playing while reserving the right to step out and resume her/his teacher role at any time.

Working in this way, once I sense an investment in the drama on the part of the children, I can challenge them by introducing a tension, a problem to overcome, a dilemma to resolve. On some occasions the group is sufficiently committed and suitably mature for me to find further ways of handing more of the power over to them so that their 'ownership' of, and responsibility for, the drama increases. This has the effect of widening the frame for their creative potential and of extending their confidence. On such occasions I am present to monitor proceedings, nudge the drama gently in a certain direction, and, most especially, to slow down the action to allow thoughts and feelings to emerge and implications and consequences to be explored. The snippet of dialogue I used at the beginning of this chapter was taken from a session where a child, as commander of a spaceship, assumed control of the group, with minimal teacher support, for long periods during the drama.

### Lesson 2: Space mission

I had been working with the junior class referred to at the beginning of this chapter in exploring the theme of emotions. Though the class worked very well I had been struck by the amount of violence being depicted, especially by the boys, in the tableau exercises I gave them to do. Many child-devised 'scenes' were straight from television, bank robberies, a gang beating up a victim‚ and so on – the sort of situation which causes the cautious class teacher to give up the idea of drama altogether.

I met this group again several weeks later. My plan for the session was to deal with gender roles and to open up the issue of violence as a male preoccupation. Inspired by some work described by O'Neill and Lambert (1982), I chose space travel as my theme. A space story would, I hoped, be sufficiently removed from the children's real experiences to provide a safe context in which to explore the issues I had in mind.

I had to plan carefully as I wanted to give the children as much ownership of the drama as possible while ensuring that I got my opportunity to challenge their thinking. I decided to take the role of an alien who traps the starship in orbit round her planet and challenges the gender mix aboard the ship. I negotiated with the children to be allowed to experiment with a space voyage. They showed immediate enthusiasm for the theme.

We had very limited hall time, so it was doubly important that I gained the children's commitment early by letting them make most of the initial choices. For instance, I asked them to decide possible reasons for the space voyage. They put forward several good ideas and then voted for 'Look for life on another planet'. The class decided that 'We, the crew, needed to find a safe place to live, to escape World War Three, which was affecting the sun, which was expected to blow up at any minute.'

The class thought the ship should have a commander. There was some initial amusement when a girl volunteered along with some boys. In the end a girl was nominated and chosen democratically by both boys and girls to lead the group. This turned out to be a wise choice which affected the eventual quality of the drama. Other roles were decided upon amicably. The class teacher was to take the role of computer expert.

After creating the ship by using blocks for the bridge and chairs, mats and available PE apparatus for the body, we had a countdown and set course for the planet Pluto where we hoped to find a life-sustaining environment. The children involved themselves in fairly free dramatic play, interrupted only by me, to narrate that we were now five months into our journey.

Life aboard the ship continued until they were again interrupted by me, now in role as the alien (speaking through a microphone for greater impact). As seen from the dialogue at the beginning of this chapter, I told the crew that their ship was being held in orbit and I questioned the commander (Jane) about the gender of the personnel aboard. The drama shifted gear when she took up my challenge and stood firm against me over the gender of the explorers. In response to her firmness, I, as the alien, was able to feed in more information for the class to work on. I expressed puzzlement that males from Earth could hold any positions of responsibility: 'On our planet, males are not intelligent enough to be given responsibility.' I asked for four females carrying different responsibilities to be beamed down to talk. Their space ship would not be allowed to land until I was reassured about the presence of males aboard.

At this point we had to return to the classroom, as the hall was in demand from another group. We decided to hold a meeting in the canteen of the ship (that was the best we could do with the tables and chairs at this point). I asked Jane if she would like to lead the meeting or would she like one of the teachers to chair it for her. She wanted to do it on her own, so we teachers took the roles of computer expert and radio operator, taking our turns with the rest of the crew to speak.

Having chosen to conduct the meeting herself, Jane showed remarkable abilities in controlling the discussion, looking for consensus and countering irrelevant suggestions.

Here are some excerpts:

> *Commander Jane*: (*to whole crew*) What do you think we should do about this?
> *Michael*: I think we should send a couple of our ships to spy and see what their planet is really like before we do any action.
> *Jane*: (*opening the discussion to the rest*) Do you think that is a good idea?
> *Jitinder*: No, I don't.
> *Jane*: Well, what do you think then?
> *Jitinder*: I think we should wait a bit and then if they send some fighter pilots then we can get our fighter pilots to destroy them in an attack.
> *Rachel*: We can't get out because we are stuck in orbit.

Rachel's logic, even though backed up by the commander, was ignored. The boys were intent on using their technological muscle in some way or other.

> *David*: We don't know what guns they've got, the size of their ships or how many they've got.

> *Mohan*: I think we should send down four females and then we
> should send them down with a fighter pilot, and station the
> fighter pilots in different places surrounding where the person
> in charge lives. And if anything happens in there, we go in.

In order to move the children on from their preoccupation with
attack and defence I used the teacher-in-role technique as one of
the crew. I pointed out that our discussion was leading us
towards the possibility of starting a war with these aliens. Was
that what we wanted? Surely we needed to settle on this planet?
The discussion then ranged from concern that our four females
might be taken hostage, to ideas of sending an animal down first
to see if it could survive, to plans to build a robot with camera
eyes to send down to survey the situation.

I asked the crew why they thought the alien didn't seem to like
males. A fighter pilot (Mohan) answered thoughtfully:

> Maybe it's because a male has committed something wrong and
> they can't trust them any more and that's happened too many
> times with the males.

The children decided that they needed more information. The
commander wished to speak again to the alien and I resumed that
role and gave her assurances that the four females beamed down
would be safe provided they were unarmed.

She chose to trust me. The group were beamed down to talk to
the alien and explained why they had come to Pluto seeking
refuge. They told me about the war on Earth and the Sun's explo-
sion and explained that scientists had caused it. I was puzzled to
discover that these scientists had been both male and female.

I explained that ours was a peaceful planet. Our aggressive
males were now under control and used only for heavy jobs and
making children. I was still reluctant to let the ship land because
of the presence of males aboard who appeared to hold equal
status with the females. The girls defended the equality of the
males in their community.

The crew members reported back to their colleagues aboard
ship and answered questions about the physical conditions on the
planet. The discussion became rather diffused at that point so we
stopped it there.

We had a chance to reflect on the drama at a later date. The
class had various ideas about ways in which the Earthlings could
prove to the alien that males and females were equal: intelligence

tests, videos of men and women living together, videos of men's jobs, inviting the aliens to visit Earth, letting a man disguise himself as a woman and after a month reveal his true identity having proved he could behave. Darren suggested an interesting test to prove that men did not need to be aggressive, the aliens could 'wind them up' and if the men remained calm, they passed the test.

I then asked the children if males and females were really equal on Earth. 'It depends *where* on Earth', said one Indian boy, immediately pointing out cultural differences. We decided to look at Britain. The children were grappling with the whole concept of equality during the discussion. Some children seemed to think equality meant sameness, so males and females were not equal, because they had different personalities and liked different activities. Women required to stay at home were not equal to the men who went out to work. Could they not be different but equal? Some children thought they could, but others were firm in their belief that the man was the head of the household.

I was fascinated to hear their perceptions of who held power in institutions other than the family. 'Ladies are the rulers' at the moment because we had a queen and a woman prime minister. The children, on being asked, did consider that there were more male MPs in Parliament than female. However, one boy argued that the power was held equally, because although there were more men in the cabinet, Margaret Thatcher was more powerful than all of them. There were many more men in the armed forces. One boy commented that women would not want to fly aeroplanes anyway. 'It's not that ladies don't want to fly aeroplanes,' Jenny observed thoughtfully, 'but men won't let them because they need to protect the children, and they're better at protecting the children.'

David pointed out that archbishops and the Pope were men in power; an example which was very relevant to our drama, though in this real case the women were the excluded group. We talked about the split between the bishops on the ordination of women. If women were not allowed in, how could they be equal?

A girl brought up the old chestnut about physical strength and male-dominated jobs. I asked her: 'If you wanted to be a builder when you grow up, could you?' She was nonplussed. Some of the girls were quite sure she couldn't. On being pushed further they said it was not because she would not be allowed to, but males always did these jobs and it would be embarrassing.

Sunil said that men owned the businesses.

David observed that in schools you do not find many men teachers which meant women were in charge (true of his school). I asked the class to think of other schools where there was a male headmaster. They had many examples to give, realizing, I hope, that the particular was not necessarily representative of the general.

I felt the discussion went well. There was no rivalry apparent between boys and girls, no polarization of views. Reflection on the drama had led to a sincere discussion and, I believe, raised some awareness. I was lucky to work with a class where the teacher had already built up an atmosphere of trust and openness where everyone's views were valued.

## Moving into theatre

Violence seems to be a theme running through this chapter, more because it insists on being there, than because at any point I planned for it. In the lesson I have just described, the class teacher and I worked in role to challenge the aggressive tendencies in the boys.

When I taught in a middle school I noticed the tendency for the boys to want to let their small-group improvisation work develop into a fight. Instead of forbidding or challenging this behaviour, I exploited it, during drama club, by creating a dance drama about a real issue that was affecting all the children in the school. Boys and girls were competing for too small a playground. Teachers on duty observed who came off worse. The older boys generally set up a football game; the football pitch, invisibly flexible, could stretch the entire length of the playground irrespective of prior claims to the space by the rest of the children. During the game the players, wonderfully gymnastic, hovered in the air or skidded gracefully to the ground. The intensity of the match was so great that the players would sacrifice almost anything to get at the ball. The sacrifice of other games, especially those of the girls, was a small price to pay for the excitement of the match.

In the drama club the children worked on their playground games, stylizing them with the use of exaggerated movements and slow motion. In addition, we did a lot of work on stage fighting, building up a fight blow by blow using different levels and parts of the body. We choreographed a scenario to be performed in the round to powerful music by Sky.

The dance drama started with the girls playing different games such as kingy (a game of tag using a ball, played in a circle) and skipping with a long imaginary rope (this had to be done at normal speed). The boys came into the scene dribbling an imaginary ball with great expertise until they caught the rope, pulling several girls to the ground. A fight between the boys and girls ensued. (The girl–boy pairs worked happily together in rehearsal, seeing that this was needed for the performance.) The fight was carefully choreographed but very convincing. The girls emerged victorious and processed triumphantly over the strewn bodies of the boys. The boys, to some very sad music, slowly got up and left the acting space nursing their wounds and bruised egos.

I imagined that we would go on to find some sort of resolution to the conflict, a division across the playground perhaps. But, in one rehearsal, the children improvised a situation where a girl waited behind after the fight to help the last boy to his feet. He shrugged her off, full of injured pride, and they went off slowly and separately each with a bowed head. We were all very moved.

'That's it', insisted the children. 'That's the end.' But didn't they want to have an enquiry, find a resolution? 'No', they insisted, that was the ending they wanted, it 'felt' right. Clearly the boys had invested so much in the dance drama as a piece of corporate creative art, that they were willing to risk their vulnerable male egos, in the eyes of a potential audience, for the greater satisfaction of getting the play artistically right. I was impressed by their integrity and the energy and commitment of the whole group.

Although the subject matter was about a conflict between boys and girls, the devising process required that both sexes worked intimately with one another. So, paradoxically, while exploring this violent theme through theatre, increased co-operation between the sexes was the outcome.

The boys' egos were again tested when the dance drama was performed to the school. The girls in the audience loved it, but some of the boys felt offended, even betrayed. They were certainly having their assumptions challenged and some interesting discussions took place later in their classrooms. All agreed it had been a good performance so the boys who took part were able to enjoy a different kind of kudos. They, after all, had displayed superb movement skills. I like to think that they had gained a good deal by being brave enough to challenge, through theatre, the collective male macho image.

That was some years ago. I wonder if my pacifist leanings and more protective drama style would allow me to encourage such a potentially violent play now. Yet I have to admit it was one of the most exciting pieces of work I have ever devised with children.


## Conclusion

Here are some comments from children who took part in the space drama:

> I think it was exciting and very real.

> I felt as though I was in a new dimension.

> We worked together in a team, and it made us feel we were really in a spaceship, not in the hall at all.

Because children are so ready to suspend their disbelief and become intellectually and emotionally involved, we teachers can offer them, through drama, 'real' experiences, in addition to those they meet in everyday life.

It is from experience, more than anything else, and reflection on that experience, that attitudes are formed. 'You can't preach experience', though as teachers we often try to. Through carefully structured drama work teachers might help to develop the kinds of attitudes that create caring, thinking, independent and responsible members of society. Drama is an ideal medium through which to explore social issues. I feel I have only just started. There is so much to do.


## Recommended reading

Davies, Geoff (1983) *Practical Primary Drama*, Heinemann.
Bolton, Gavin (1984) *Drama as Education*, Longman.
O'Neill, Cecily, Lambert, Alan, Linnell, Rosemary and Warr-Wood, Janet (1977) *Drama Guidelines*, Heinemann.

# CHAPTER 4

# Design and Technology in the Primary Classroom: Equalizing Opportunities

## BRIDGET EGAN

*Stereotypical assumptions about design and technology and about girls' and boys' needs in this area of the curriculum affect the expectations and behaviour of both teachers and pupils. This chapter attempts to explore the differing attitudes of boys and girls to written and practical work in schools.*

> CDT? It's very important that we get it off the ground in our school; especially for our boys.

Ten years after the main body of equal opportunities legislation was enacted in Britain, a primary school deputy head teacher finds nothing strange in her statement quoted above. When it is pointed out to her that children of both sexes will be involved in working on design-and-make projects, she repeats: 'Yes, I know girls do it, too; but it's *more important for the boys.*' Another colleague says 'Of course, the girls are much less interested than the boys.' It is far from uncommon for established teachers to express such beliefs, and many also believe that boys perform better than girls in primary school design-and-make activities.

By contrast, many teachers committed to reducing the inequity that is visible in young peoples' curriculum choices at secondary level believe that the involvement of girls at primary school in CDT projects will result in more girls choosing to pursue technical and scientific options in later schooling, because they believe that lack of early experience is a significant factor in deterring girls from becoming involved to any great extent in CDT at later stages. Against this latter view, it must be pointed out that experience of an area of the curriculum does not of itself necessarily reduce such inequities of choices. Science and maths options at secondary level continue to be dominated, particularly at A level, by boys, despite equality of early experience and high success rates for girls at earlier stages of schooling. There is no reason to suggest that simply eliminating the differential extent of early experience will significantly alter the rates at which girls opt for design-related subjects later on. It is possible, however, that reducing the differential in *quality* of experience may do so.

The investigation of discriminatory non-curricular practices in primary schools which may have a 'knock-on' effect on the child's understanding of her/his relationship to the curriculum is well documented. I propose to examine two aspects of attitudes in Western industrial society which interact to produce an effect on the perception of certain curriculum areas, notably those such as maths, science and CDT which demand active learning procedures.

In addition, I intend to discuss some features of CDT teaching which may significantly affect the way in which girls and boys perceive it.

### Socialization and conformity

Child-rearing practices in the Western world are largely concerned with persuading children to conform to adult expectations of behaviour. Socialization into the world of school stresses conformity to a whole series of norms which children are unlikely to have met previously. Young children experiencing school for the first time are expected to learn a large number of rules of behaviour appropriate to membership of a community wider than hitherto encountered. Social approval from powerful adults (such as teachers and dinner controllers) is earned by conforming to these norms, and social success measured and rewarded according to the speed with which conformity is achieved. It is frequently the case, however, that these demands are not clearly articulated in ways that the children can understand. Learning proceeds often by trial and error, and behavioural goals all too often remain inexplicit.

The cliché that 'boys will be boys' represents a view, still widely held, that it is inappropriate to expect as great an acceptance of behavioural norms from boys as from girls. At school, as in society, boys are permitted to cross the boundaries of acceptable behaviour both more frequently and with greater tolerance than are girls. Girls, therefore, learn more quickly than boys to adopt the rule-conforming attitudes of the community, and feel a stronger pressure, in school, to seek teacher approval.

Where norms remain inexplicit, children who have learnt to conform are likely to adopt 'safe' behaviours; that is, they will conform to the norms that they have heard expressed elsewhere. In an environment where the majority of the child's time is directed by the teacher, this may well account for the tendency of children to make gender-stereotyped role-conforming choices when given a 'free-choice' activity time. It will also explain why there is evidence that the experience of school, far from freeing children from pressure to make such choices according to stereotype, seems rather to reinforce it.

## The concept of 'work'

A feeling still exists among many teachers, as well as among parents and other interested parties, that 'work' in the context of school consists mainly of sitting at a table and writing. There are strong reasons for the persistence of this attitude. The more traditional tasks of school – reading, writing and numeracy practice – are all activities which are essentially measurable. They are susceptible to marking procedures, and it is relatively easy, therefore, to monitor a child's progress in these skills, and to have a clear picture of what is being learnt at any given time. Active learning situations, on the other hand, are relatively difficult to assess. What is being learnt is, in the short term, more diffuse, and may not correspond to the teacher's original intentions in devising the task. Nor is it as easy to see when a child is 'on task' as it would be if the child were desk-bound: the teacher cannot be certain without making a detailed check whether the child is engaged on the task in hand, or giving the majority of its attention to non-task activities.

Time scales are also less well defined. When the child is given charge of its own learning, it is less possible for the teacher to demand that a task is completed in a given time. It is hardly remarkable if parents and children, and some teachers, learn to attach greater importance to activities that are time-defined and easily assessed, and in which success can be clearly demonstrated and measured, than to those that are otherwise.

It is also interesting to note that when children make models, or do artwork, these pieces of work are typically taken home either on completion or after a short time on display, whereas written work remains at school after completion, and the teacher exercises discretion about whether or not it goes home at the end of a term or year. For most teachers, of course, this is a response to the logistical problem of storage in the limited space of the average primary classroom, but it may well be that children receive a different message, also to do with the status of the work. Art and craft work is the property of the child, whereas written work is, and may remain, the property of the school. In our society, children's property is accorded a lower value than that of adults, which in turn has a lower status than that of institutions. This once again ensures that the products of the more traditional activities of school are valued more highly than those of active learning.

That this stereotype of 'work' is powerfully transmitted within the culture is demonstrated by the way in which young children perceive the activities that they are asked to engage in at school. The children quoted below do not in any way constitute a statistical sample of the population. All are, however, both intelligent and articulate, and have extensive experience of nursery schooling. All come from professional middle-class homes, and their parents are keenly interested in their schooling. One would expect these children, therefore, to be exceptionally well informed about the world of school, rather than the reverse. Their answers are, therefore, indicative. Each child was interviewed at home. The interview began with general discussion about school, and the focus on 'work' was not introduced until the child first used the word.

Simon is an only child of four years and nine months. He is due to start infant school one week after his next birthday, at the beginning of the new term. He currently attends nursery school full-time.

*BE*: What will you do at your new school?
*Simon*: Hard work.

*BE*: What hard work will you do?
*Simon*: Writing . . . and we will do . . . be good.

Asked if 'being good' is part of the work he will do, Simon replies that it is hard, but not 'work': 'you just do it so you don't go in the corner' [*sic!*].

Further enquiry elicits no more information about 'work', and indeed, Simon's expectations of school are somewhat hazy, but he describes his 'work' at nursery as playing indoors, whereas playing out of doors constitutes 'play'.

Katia is just five, and will join her older sister at primary school in about ten weeks' time, when the new term starts. She attends a private nursery school full-time. She too has a clear idea that school involves work.

*BE*: What will you do when you go to school?
*Katia*: Lots of work . . . Maths, reading, writing . . . I've got a reading book . . .
*BE*: Is there any other work that you'll do?
*Katia*: I don't know.
*BE*: Will you be doing other things at school as well as work?
*Katia*: Yes . . . Playing on the computer, watching telly . . . um . . . playing.
*BE*: What sort of playing, do you think?
*Katia*: Lego?
*BE*: And is that work?
*Katia*: No.

Further discussion explored Katia's favourite play activities. When she mentioned drawing, crayoning and painting, I asked if she thought she might do those things at school.

*Katia*: I *know* I'll do painting.
*BE*: Will that be work?
*Katia*: No. That's playing.

Julia is five years and three months old. She joined her elder brother at primary school three weeks ago, at the start of term, having previously attended a nursery class attached to a different primary school.

*BE*: Will you tell me about the things you do at school?
*Julia*: Work in my number book. And maths . . .
*BE*: What other work do you do?
*Julia*: We do singing in the Hall . . . and . . . mm . . . we go to Assembly . . .

*BE*: Do you do other things that aren't work?
*Julia*: Assembly isn't work.

The conversation roams for a while, and then comes back to school. Julia introduces the fact that she reads at school.

*BE*: What about that? Is reading work?
*Julia*: The one that you've already had and you've brought back from your house and you go to school with it in your reading book bag and read it to the teacher and then you give it back and she puts it in her reading book place where she puts them . . .
*BE*: Is that work?
*Julia*: Yes. And we do drawing sometimes. That isn't work.
*BE*: Do you do anything else?
*Julia*: Sometimes . . . sometimes she says it's clearing up time . . .
*BE*: And is that work?
*Julia*: Yes (*laughs*).

James is also in his third week at primary school. He is the eldest child in his family, and was at the same nursery as Simon until the end of last term. He is very clear in the distinction he draws between 'work' and other school activities.

*BE*: What do you do at school?
*James*: Number . . . writing . . . talking about the children; the children do their work . . . they work still . . . and all the children have to work 'cause it's a long long time to go home.
*BE*: What else do you do?
*James*: Playing . . . and we build a wall and hide behind it.
*BE*: When you build a wall, is that work?
*James*: No, it's playing; and all the other toys are playing.
*BE*: What toys do you have in your classroom?
*James*: Sand, a train track, bridges, and something else . . . toys.
*BE*: And when you use those things, is that work?
*James*: Well, when you've done all your work you can play with them. That's a treat.

James also mentions as 'work' two further activities, which he refers to as 'practical' and 'activities'. He does not know what is meant by either of these terms, and says that he has never participated in either.

It is by no means uncommon, even now, for some teachers to use some activities, such as the sand tray in James's classroom, as motivators to persuade children who otherwise show little interest to engage in what is seen as 'real' work. Even when the teacher has a firm commitment to active learning, this traditional attitude may be hard to shake off. The activities chosen as reinforcers tend to be those such as art and CDT, which are pupil-directed and intrinsically rewarding. How often has a teacher been heard to say, 'Until you have finished that model, I can't let you do your number work'?

It is well established (Whyte, 1983, ch. 3) that girls in general perform better at primary school in all areas of the curriculum than do boys. This means that they are less likely than boys to be offered the rewarding activities such as CDT as an inducement to become involved with work. Since they are also under greater pressure to conform and to earn teacher approval, they are less likely to take an interest in low-status activities such as CDT.

## Equalizing opportunity

Another factor which has been alleged to affect girls' willingness to participate in CDT is the frequency with which teachers choose to use themes such as 'Transport' as a starting point for CDT. Many teachers believe that the association of such themes with play activities traditionally ascribed to boys (such as using toy cars and boats, and model-making from kits) may well put many girls off.

While it is true that some teachers may not have considered the full range of possible topic options to develop understanding of mechanical concepts, there is no evidence to suggest that girls find it more difficult than boys to come to grips with such topics. Martin Grant's (1984) research findings, from work with secondary school pupils, suggest rather that the context of the design brief is the important factor. Presenting briefs as a search for relevant solutions to real human problems had a greater effect on girls' interest and involvement than searching for 'girl-friendly' topics. Since the majority of primary school teachers organize children's learning around themes or topics, it is not difficult to present briefs in this way.

Pupils and teachers not infrequently perceive boys as performing better at CDT than girls. One reason for this may be the greater confidence with which boys tackle design-and-make activities. If the teacher is herself lacking in experience of and confidence in the use of tools and materials, she may well mistake confidence in this area for competence.

The facts may well be otherwise. I have frequently observed that the girl who has not 'done it with my dad, Miss' performs better with saw, drill and hammer than the boy who has had a go, but not been taught to use the tools efficiently. His confidence becomes a barrier to learning rather than an aid. Moreover, boys, thinking themselves on familiar territory, may find it more difficult to think around a design brief and engage in creative planning, because their confidence leads them to think that they know what is required.

Because they tend to be less confident about their success in this area of the curriculum, girls need correspondingly more encouragement and praise for their efforts if they are to experience success. Again, this may involve a change in behaviour by the teacher, who may be more accustomed to recognizing boys' need for encouragement (in the more traditional subjects) than girls'.

Also important is the provision of competent female role models, as it is at secondary level. At present, a disproportionately high number of posts of responsibility for CDT are held by men. A significantly higher percentage of places on long in-service training courses are taken up by men than would be indicated by their representation in primary schools. If CDT is seen, at primary as at secondary school, as being the province of men, the effect will be that girls distance themselves from the activity at an earlier age.

Removing CDT from the margins of 'real' work is clearly another important strategy in ensuring equal opportunity. Action needs to be taken by teachers, either in the way in which briefs are presented, or in the ways in which teaching areas are organized and managed, to ensure that CDT tasks are fully integrated into the curriculum, and that expectations of performance and completion are as high as for the more traditional tasks. Materials such as construction kits should not be left simply as free-choice activities, nor as a reward for achievement in another curriculum area, but be accompanied by some brief, and the expectation should be that every child uses the material at some stage during a normal working week.

By demarginalizing CDT, and by raising its 'work' status, by providing competent female role models, and by counteracting girls' lack of confidence in this area of work, a major change in the traditional attitudes of girls may be possible.

## Further reading

Catton, J. (1985) *Ways and Means: The Craft, Design and Technology Education of Girls*, Longman (for SCDC).
Down, B. (1986) *'CDT and Equal Opportunities' Studies in Design Education, Craft and Technology*, vol. 19, no. 1.
EOC (1983) *Do you provide Equal Opportunities?*
Sharpe, S. (1976) *Just Like a Girl*, Penguin.
Stanworth, M. (1983) *Gender and Schooling*, Hutchinson.

## Note

Since the writing of this chapter, Micro Electronic Support Unit (MESU) have also published material suggesting that attitudes to "work" have significance in influencing girls' choice of subject, (see MESU, 'Participation of Girls in the New Technologies', press release, 18 March 1988).

# CHAPTER 5

# The Use of Construction Kits to Foster Equal Opportunity, CDT, and Collaborative Learning

## JO SHERWIN

*Teachers often ask for practical suggestions, based on experience, in helping young girls to feel more confident with construction kits. This account of one teacher's success in working with children in a reception class can easily be modified and used by others.*

During 1986–7, as a curriculum support teacher in a Slough first school, I was given the opportunity to develop an area of the curriculum. In order to foster gender equality, I chose to concentrate on CDT. The idea for this project was generated as a result of discussion with other members of staff involved in in-service training courses in equal opportunities at our local teachers' centre. At one of these sessions two women teachers from Brent showed us how they used construction kits in order to demonstrate in a practical way to girls that they need not obey the social dictum that girls have dolls and boys have bricks; that roles can be interchanged; that girls can and should gain satisfaction by building something in three dimensions; that engineering for girls can be fun and stimulating. In addition to this, I thought it would be a good way into CDT for children aged from five to eight. Prior to this, CDT had already been given a higher profile in our LEA. Many of us went on courses where we learnt to construct various objects. However, no mention was made of the way in which this activity would or could broaden and extend the curriculum. I took one whole day to build a small balsawood and card cart – and came away discouraged. Teachers are so busy and the curriculum seems continually to diversify, that the thought of assembling all the materials, keeping up the stock, millions of gluey fingers and fragile broken carts seemed beyond the mental and physical capabilities of many of us. So we opted for a guilty silence, an 'I know I should, but . . .' sort of stance.

The teachers from Brent introduced us to construction kits. Colourful, easy to handle for small fingers, the finished product would look good, and was easily obtainable (if expensive) on the open market and *durable*. Most kits come with plenty of building ideas, and brainstorming in staff meetings produced yet more. The possibilities for collaborative learning came later, after I had begun to work with the children.

Now I had to think about organizing the materials. To this end I made a visit to the Brent schools, Wykeham Primary and Mora Infants, whose teachers had first given me the idea. They showed me what they were doing and gave me hints on how to organize myself, the work and my resources. When I write about how I went about the task I speak only for myself and my situation. There are no hard and fast rules and the actual means of going about the job will differ as schools and teacher time differs. In other words, you do what is possible in your situation.

Most of the classrooms in my school had the rudiments of some new (and some ancient!) construction kits. The school was divided into three age bands of three or four classes each. I decided to provide each year band with its own stock of construction kits, stored in crates light enough for children to carry. The Brent (1986) booklet, *Design it, Build it, Use it!*, evaluates the more useful kits. We ordered six or seven different lots of construction kits for each unit. In the end each unit had a library of six crates stored in the corridor central to the unit classrooms. Children could be sent to fetch a particular crate, or indeed choose one as they wished.

Now my classroom work began. As the Brent teachers suggested, in the initial stages (one term, more or less) I worked only with girls. We cannot talk about equal opportunities unless girls are as confident and as knowledgeable as boys appear to be. It is partly the boys' display of confidence that makes the girls feel inadequate in this area of the curriculum. I had a list of girls in each classroom and for each session I took a mixed-ability group of four girls for one hour, usually within the classroom, throughout the school. It should be remembered that I was a support teacher for the year, and a single-class teacher would probably not have a whole hour to spend with a group of children and so would have to think in terms of alternative organization. Nevertheless, I feel it is important to work with girls in the first instance.

For the first two sessions the girls worked on individual items – at times slightly directed – such as 'things on wheels' or 'things that fly'. This encouraged them to make cars, trucks, bicycles, birds, aeroplanes and butterflies from the beginning. Despite possible accusations of reinforcing stereotypical perspectives, I decided not to stop girls from making houses. But just as teachers discourage the constant repetition of 'I went to the park', or 'I went to the shops' in young children's story writing, and suggest a more exciting variation for a story, I would suggest and direct girls towards other things after 'the house' had been made more than once. Sometimes we went out for a walk to look for things we might make. The girls chose their own kits, gradually learning through discussion and practical experience to select the appropriate kit for their particular task.

Then we began to work in pairs. This was not easy at first. Many girls insisted on working on their own individual items. Co-operation is in itself a skill that has to be learned and teaches the value of your own and others' opinions.

At the same time I made stand-up name cards for each child; after each session the girls would find their card and put it on or beside their model, which remained on display in the classroom until the next session the following week. This fostered pride and a sense of importance in the girls. During the session the girls either painted a picture of their model or, at another session, made a model of it using other materials, wrote a story about it, told a story on tape about it, or how to make it; some acted out a story using their model. In other words, there was always some follow-up, which was also displayed, or in the case of a tape, played to the class, or at an assembly; and, as I shall show later, more often than not, some forward planning, too, in the form of designs or cartoons.

The girls' manipulative skills improved apace and after each girl had worked for two sessions as part of a pair I began to ask them to work as a group. Before starting this phase of work it seemed appropriate to link into a topic or project theme that the children were working on in their classrooms. I had consulted with my colleagues in their unit meetings and they had come up with lots of ideas as to what would be relevant to the topic of the moment. For instance, for a topic on clothes we made a clothes horse, a rack to dry clothes on, shoe boxes, hat boxes, 'fantastic' hats. For a topic on animals we made enclosures for animals – a lion cage, bird cage, aquarium, using other materials such as plasticine, straws and bits of wood. A topic on 'homes' lent itself to the designing of flats, houses, caravans, houseboats, and so on. By the time I was working with four girls as a team, the collaborative aspect of the work was being refined and extended. The group discussed and designed the proposed construction, made it and then chose an appropriate follow-up activity. When the girls had worked for two sessions as a team, in my view it was time to start with mixed groups. By now, the boys had begun to make a lot of noise about being left out.

I began again as I had with the girls; a mixed-ability group of four, two boys and two girls. The only difference was that we were now alerted to each class or unit's topic theme, so the design, making and follow-up were directed to that. I ran two sessions of individual work with each group so that the girls would have a chance to establish their competence and not succumb to the boys' feelings of superiority about their abilities in the construction field. Previously, the boys had perceived it their right not only to have the construction kit but also the space in which to work; they gradually elbowed the girls out. Now the girls refused to budge.

Name cards were made for everyone so that all work was validated when on display. These two initial sessions led to the 'crunch' stage: mixed pairs! The choice was to leave the group or to work in mixed pairs. Amid wary looks, sheepish and embarrassed grins, much hesitation, and some outright refusals, the mixed pairs were accepted. The girls did not fall into the passive role and definitely held their own with the boys. In fact in many cases they had the edge because they were already used to working towards a definite end.

It was at this stage that the talk was the most fascinating; terminology and sharing of ideas developed speedily: 'Where's the Phillips screwdriver?', 'We need a strut to strengthen the roof', etc. The mixed groups continued for the rest of the school year

and, at times, even developed into 'unit' or school working
groups or for exhibitions of work. For example, at Christmas the
lower unit built the hotel where Mary and Joseph did *not*
go – complete with swimming pool! The middle group made the
stars, angels and animals for the stable, while the upper unit
made the people (plasticine), their clothes, the crib and the stable.
On another occasion the upper unit made a fairground for their
topic on 'energy', making links with a television programme they
were watching – a 'thriller' about a fairground. For Guru Nanak's
birthday, two girls and two boys sketched a Gurdwara, a Sikh
temple. They then made a construction model of the temple.
When it was completed it was taken to a parallel class where a
group of girls and boys, using it for reference, made a 'junk'
model of the Gurdwara.

At this stage a couple of teachers noticed that when the children
had free choice of activity more girls chose construction kits and
they were not chased away or dominated by the boys. It was also
reported that the girls were more purposeful and imaginative
about the models they made while the boys were still making
weapons. A few girls had begun by saying 'I can't', but by half-
way through the year those words were not heard again except
from girls in the new reception intake. It began to be accepted
that this is what we *did* and we all could be more or less successful, depending upon what we were doing.

It is unlikely that a simple curriculum intervention of this kind
can result in radically altered perspectives *vis-à-vis* male–female
roles but I do believe we can sow seeds so that when children,
especially girls, make choices in life they are not bound by rigidly
and stereotypically defined role expectations.

As an integral resource to go with this work, I made some work
cards. These could be used as either teacher or child resource. In
discussions the staff formulated lots of problem-solving ideas.
One was: 'There is a busy road running between a school and an
adventure playground. How can the children safely cross the
road? Build the school, the road, the adventure playground, and
the "safe passage".' Another: 'Build something to support the
weight of this stone.' Still another: 'Build something strong
enough to pull this stone.' Such ideas were put onto graded cards
and placed in a storage box for each age band. For this storage
box I also made more colourful work cards. Some of these had
pictures from the boxes in which the construction kit came. These

were cut out and glued onto card with written instructions or suggestions. On other cards I put photographs of children with their models. The children were named and in this way both they and the activity were celebrated. For example: 'Shahida has made a cube using straws and plasticine. Can you make another solid shape? How many sides has your shape got? What materials did you use?'

Alongside this construction work, each class was furnished with a 'tinker box'. This was another suggestion made by the teachers in Brent. A tinker box is simply a plastic container furnished with a hammer, hacksaw, two or three types of screwdriver' pliers, screws, nails and a plane – which must be removed and used only under close supervision. The children were asked to bring in oddments, such as old pieces of wood, old clocks, hairdryers, radios. One child even staggered in with an ancient till. With these things the children were encouraged to do exactly as the name suggests – to 'tinker'. I showed about eight or ten children in each class how to use the tools safely and they in turn taught others in their class. Both boys and girls loved 'tinkering' as a free-choice activity. Safety and sanity dictate that it should be chosen by no more than four children at a time.

Although more complicated technical kits may be more attractive to some teachers, in my view, money spent on advanced kits will be wasted unless the children have fully explored the more basic kits and their possibilities and are conceptually ready for the more complex kits. The next stage is more technologically complicated and teachers will need to spend considerable time learning about them before presenting them to the children. Furthermore, the children will now need substantial teacher time.

In order for CDT and equal opportunities to have any real impact, the classroom teacher will have to timetable such activities as she/he would any other curriculum area in an integrated day. It is well worth the effort to see some girls' expressions or bodies saying proudly: 'I am a girl. I *can*.'

# CHAPTER 6

# Deepa's Story: Writing Non-Sexist Stories for a Reception Class

## CHRISTINA SHAMARIS

*Young children all enjoy fiction, but good non-sexist stories are still scarce. Christina Shamaris describes the effects on her fourth-year secondary GCSE group of writing, illustrating and reading such stories for a neighbouring reception class.*

The idea of writing anti-sexist stories for infants originally came from Sue D'Arcy, a teacher from our neighbouring first school. I was aware of her commitment to developing and carrying out anti-sexist teaching strategies, and also that she was very keen to collaborate with teachers and pupils from another school to see what effect that might have on her class.

The school where I teach is a girls' secondary school where many of the pupils are Muslim. When Sue first mentioned the idea in 1986, I lacked the confidence to address gender issues. I was wary of offending any cultural codes and thought it best to avoid doing so. Since then the ethos of the school has gradually begun to change. There is a new headteacher who is committed to offering her pupils equality of opportunity so that they can face the outside world with confidence based on realistic expectations.

The group with whom I chose to work, in collaboration with another English teacher, Margaret Taylor, on this project was my fourth-year GCSE English group. In order to show the value of this work for the teachers and pupils from both schools, I shall describe the process by which the writing of their stories was achieved, and how these were accepted by the first school children. Using extracts from transcripts of taped conversations with our pupils, and from their written work, I analyse some of the stories to support my own interpretation of the project.

## Our aims

Our aims for the project were many and varied but all equally important. They fell broadly into three areas. First, we wished to develop in the girls an awareness and understanding of gender issues in schools and in the world around them. Here are some comments made by the girls at the end of the project:

> *Anita*: I never really thought about girls and boys being different, it would just be natural that girls get that – and boys get that.
> *Roji*: Yeah, it's the way you get brought up.
> *Anita*: Yeah – but I never bothered about it really – 'cause it never came out.
> *Teacher*: Do you feel slightly more bothered about it now?
> *Anita*: Yes – very.

Second, the stories should be readable and well written. Writing for a critical young audience would be different from writing for teachers or examiners. Finally we wanted the girls to analyse the writing process. We realized that writing stories for a specific audience of five- to six-year-olds, stories which both promoted the issue of gender equality and which captured the interest and imagination of the audience, was a complex task. The process the girls underwent to achieve it will be described in more detail later, along with some of their own comments.

We also wished to develop certain skills which we hoped would result from the first two aims: to develop the pupils' imaginative and creative faculties and to encourage language development in reading, writing and talking, and also to give status to home languages. We hoped the pupils would use some Asian characters in their stories, particularly as the class for which they were writing was of a similar racial mix to their own. So, often Asian pupils write themselves out of stories, appearing to feel more comfortable with names like Jane, Jim or Jason rather than Kulvinder or Avtar. We were hoping to persuade them to give greater validity to their own experiences and life-styles by writing about people that both the authors and the reception class children would recognize and respond to with confidence.

As each pupil would be working with a partner we were hoping to develop a positive attitude towards negotiation, co-operation, organization of tasks and responsibility. As authors, the pupils would also be developing critical and analytical skills necessary for the selection and shaping of their ideas.

The stories were to be illustrated, bound and written in a style appropriate to five- and six-year-olds, so our pupils would also need to develop the required technical and presentational skills. They would need to choose appropriate lettering and to work out how to arrange words and illustrations on a page. The books were to be properly bound using a ring binder. This comment from one of the pupils, Jasbir, reports on how she and her partner worked together.

> The next stage was to put the whole book together. We had a few ups and downs, but we managed to put it as one whole book. We had to plan how we were going to set the pages out and we decided to have a page of writing and a page of pictures . . . Then we had to decide on a cover. I thought of the idea of the cover, and my partner designed it, because I am not good at drawing. At this stage we had a lot of decision-making to do, it was hard because we had different opinions, but we came to an agreement at the end.

We also wanted to develop our pupils' confidence in a number of ways. Oral confidence was important, as the girls were to read their own stories aloud to the children for whom they had been written, and to encourage discussion on the issues raised by the project. Then we hoped to develop self-confidence and self-esteem by giving genuine status to the stories, by publishing them and entering the books in the school library. Hameeda later wrote:

> When we saw our book made it looked excellent, we were really pleased with it. It looked like a *real* children's story book.

## Learning about gender issues

Margaret Taylor and I agreed that the girls had to be fully committed to the project as we were setting them a very hard task. We were also conscious of the difficulty of measuring what is actually being learnt, when tackling gender issues through writing. There was a danger that the whole business of writing and illustrating would take over and the main purpose of the initiative would get lost. Their involvement in one process would allow the girls to remain unaffected by the very issues they were attempting to raise with their readers. However, we found that the very act of collaborative writing and the amount of discussion it necessitated led to constant references to sexism and its damaging effects. We decided to lend status to the work by introducing Eva Tutchell as a guest, an expert who would be working with us for a few weeks. Eva began the project by leading an awareness-raising workshop highlighting equal opportunities, gender issues and sexism in schools. We decided not to tell the pupils that their work would be to write anti-sexist stories until later. After that initial session, Angela wrote:

> What I understand by 'Equal Opportunities' is that girls can do everything like boys. But only if girls get a chance.

## Reading and talking about children's fiction

The next task was to alert the girls to sexism in children's stories and to introduce their job of writing non-sexist children's stories. In order to do this we asked them to assess what makes a successful children's story.

The lesson began with Eva reading *'The Paper Bag Princess'* (Munsch, 1982) to the group, a very lively, funny, anti-sexist fairy story. They were then shown extracts from a well-known reading scheme. Pictures of the boy helping father with traditionally male activities were shown, while the girl was helping mother to make tea in the kitchen. Much heated discussion concerning the role of men and women in the home followed and the girls began to make connections between fiction and life.

They began to be convinced of the need for young children to read books which presented boys and girls less stereotypically. It was at this point we told them that for the next few weeks they would be attempting to write their own anti-sexist children's stories, for a specific class of five- to six-year-olds. We explained how important and special these books would be, and that they would eventually read their stories themselves to the children. Many of the girls looked at us in disbelief, but we assured them that the enthusiasm and interest they had already displayed would see them through what seemed now to be a somewhat daunting proposition. This is what Yasmin wrote some time later:

> At first I was confused, but after discussing it I understood it much better . . . I think that it is a really good idea to write a book on equal opportunities. This was because I thought of *my infancy*, we were *also* taught only boys can play football and help Dad in making things, in those books there was not one part where a girl had as equal an opportunity as a boy.

Eva acted as liaison between the two schools and brought in the books and stories that the children at the first school said they enjoyed the most. While considering the personally chosen favourite stories of the first school children, there was much reminiscing of their own childhood favourites. The girls decided that animals of all sorts were very popular, that humour, adventure and active characters were important, but the plot should not be too complicated. They stressed the need for *suspense*: children must want to carry on reading to see what happens next. Strong moral messages, an appropriately happy ending, interesting names for characters including Asian names, strongly defined characters, bright colourful pictures, easy words and large writing were all necessary ingredients for a 'good read'.

This was an important part of the process as they began to be aware of the power of storytelling and began to recognize the author's role. Some pupils were aware of the sexism in some of the favourite books selected by the infants. For instance, Bicky later observed that even some stories about animals were sexist:

> We read two or three children's books and we were saying even if they were animals, you know male and female, they do the same things as boys and girls.

Among the selection were some books with Asian and Afro-Caribbean characters, and one written in Urdu. The girls were working in pairs and during this activity Nita asked Eva: 'Would you mind if we wrote a story in Punjabi, Hindi and English?' Naturally Eva was delighted. We had hoped that some of the girls would use Asian names and characters in their stories, and this was referred to by some of the girls in the discussion which followed. However, Nita's rather self-effacing request clearly shows how unsure she was about the status of her own language.

Was the ethos of the school, i.e. the hidden curriculum, perpetuating the idea that English was far superior to any other language – and any other culture? That question and its implications, however, could fill a book of its own. Our immediate concern was to encourage the girls to depict cultural diversity in their stories, particularly as several of the children for whom they were writing spoke fluent Punjabi, and a few were just beginning to speak English. One of the girls who was responsible for writing the triple text story had this to say in her essay:

> I chose Nita for my partner. Nita and I decided to do something different. We decided to write a story in three languages, Hindi, Punjabi and English. Then we asked Mrs Tutchell if we can write it like this or not. She was very glad . . .

Nita herself wrote:

> I had an idea of writing the book in triple text. The point we wanted to cover was that the school we were going to read the book to was not one with only English children. Many of the infants didn't understand English very well. Mrs Tutchell said it would be very useful and it would fulfil every need of a child who couldn't enjoy his school life because of not being able to understand a language. After all this we decided to do our best in everything. From there it created a great deal of interest in me.

## Writing their own stories

Observing the girls discussing their own ideas with a partner in order to decide whether to continue to produce a joint story or an individual one, we were aware of the remarkable commitment and enthusiasm already displayed. They were learning how to negotiate effectively and developing their imaginative and literary skills at the same time. We are convinced that this was because they were writing for a real identifiable audience. As Jasbir wrote later: 'We never made this book for nothing. We had to read it to the children.'

The girls experienced very real authorial pangs through the writing and producing of the stories. It was not merely that the story itself had to be written, but each was to be properly bound and presented. Therefore the girls had to consider the complete structure, including the layout, size of writing, the pictures, colours and vocabulary to be used. The following comments illustrate something of the painful process the girls underwent – and their final pleasure on the completion of the task:

> *Noreen*: The most difficult part for me was in choosing what story to write.
> *Anita*: . . . it sounded effortless, easy! When the time came to actually think out the story it was very difficult, hard and . . . sometimes . . . interminable.
> *Yasmin*: Although I was really interested . . . I found it really difficult.

Yasmin later said, however: 'I felt really pleased when my partner and I got the storyline.' Julia said: 'On TV adverts it's always a girl that's playing with a doll, and then when it's an action man or a car it's always a boy . . . So in our story it was a girl's birthday and she was given things you wouldn't expect a girl to have, like trains.'

We had discussed earlier the ways in which stereotyping usually presents males as strong and unemotional: 'Boys don't cry'. Roji and Yasmin clearly decided to address this issue in their story. They also decided to use a unisex name 'Terry' for one of their girl characters. They were hoping that the reader might be surprised to learn later that Terry was a girl even though she was sailing a toy boat. Here is an extract from their story:

> In the park you can see John and Nasif flying their kite and Terry and Satinder sailing their boat on the pond.
> James takes John's kite and breaks it, that makes John very sad and he cries.

It was interesting and reassuring to hear how the girls had negotiated and co-operated with one another during the writing. Yasmin describes how she and her partner worked together:

> We both wrote a story, then we read each other's stories, then we changed bits, we sort of combined both of them.

Nita describes here something of her working process with her partner:

> everyone was using a boy and a girl or a princess or prince. We thought of using animals. Our story's title was 'Copy Monkeys' . . . sorting out sentences which were easy and understandable to children and drawing the pictures to match was rather a difficult task, but we managed.

Time was running out but of fourteen books only two were not fully completed in time for the date set for the reading. We even managed to fit in time for the girls to practise reading aloud into a tape recorder, something which many of them found very difficult to do.

### Reading to the children

Our pupils read in pairs, taking it in turn, so that the reactions of the children could be observed. The children were in groups of about four, each group rotating so as to be able to hear as many of the stories as possible. Naturally the children were very excited at the arrival of the teenage visitors and our pupils had a difficult task to hold their interest, while so much was going on around them. Our pupils' experiences and observations that morning were varied and they themselves made illuminating comments about them. The authors of the triple-text story, 'Copy Monkeys', wrote:

> the children were very happy when we told them that we wrote this story in three languages.

> I was very pleased that the children liked it. One of them even said, 'every book should be like this', not because *he* did not understand English, but his fellow students did not.

Very different observations were made by Roji and Yasmin, who were clearly shocked by the sexism they had encountered in six-year-old children.

> *Yasmin*: We were explaining about fixing the kite or something and the boy said: 'Oh look, the girl's actually fixing the kite.'
> *Roji*: Yes, he said it couldn't be happening.
> *Yasmin*: It shouldn't be happening, honestly!
> *Roji*: He said that it was wrong, that can't happen. We said to him, 'Why?' He said: 'Girls just aren't allowed to, girls are *second*.' We said, 'No. We've got the same chances as you.'

Another girl, Hameeda, had written that in her story, 'The Lonely Princess',

> the boys didn't really like the idea of a princess rescuing her own prince. The girls thought they couldn't do the same jobs as the boys. We told them they could and they were surprised.

Because one of their central concerns in writing the stories was gender equality, many of our pupils found themselves trying to 'convert' the children in a quite didactic manner. Some of the stories took the idea of boys and girls playing with toys which are traditionally seen as male, or of showing boys helping mum and girls helping dad. These stories were not quite so popular with the children. The anti-sexist message had to be couched in stories which appealed to the imaginative inner fantasy world of the pupils (Walkerdine, 1984).

Therefore one of the most popular stories was 'The Princess and the Monster', because it took the mode of a traditional fairy tale. The story concerns the beautiful Princess Zoe captured by 'a fat green hairy monster'; 'but Zoe was brave and did not cry'.

Many of the stories, like this one, featured a girl as the central character. This seemed to be one way for our pupils to address the equal opportunities question.

Another feature of the most popular stories was the inclusion of lovable animals, as in 'Bonzo Saves the Day' and 'A Loving Surprise'. In the former the danger of talking to strangers was a central message. In the latter, Deepa, the central character, is bored. Her mother offers her 'a large doll, a pram, or a massive teddy bear'. Deepa refuses and is still bored. She is thus seen to be rejecting traditionally 'girly' toys. Her boredom is finally overcome by the acquisition, from a pet shop, of an unhappy dragon called Spiky.

## Some conclusions

The success of the project relied heavily on the collaboration between the teachers involved, a venture which may not easily be established in every school.

The number of girls in both classes was relatively low so that we could easily teach them together in one room. Three teachers in one classroom is a luxury in terms of the individual attention every pupil is able to receive. We were able to help the girls in different ways. Margaret Taylor took over all the practical side of the work, making suggestions on layout, illustrations and binding, which left me free as a drama teacher, to develop the girls' skills in reading the stories aloud in a way which would engage the attention of very young children.

But what did we learn from the project? For myself, I came to grips with the difficult problem of raising gender issues with girls, many of whom are Moslems. I now have the confidence to see that it is my duty to alert my pupils to the choices available to them. This greater confidence and awareness has also influenced my drama teaching: the following term I ran a very similar project with my fourth-year CSE drama group, where the aim was to produce a non-sexist play for infant children.

As for the children, we do know that they enjoyed the stories, but it is difficult to assess how far we were successful in raising their awareness of gender issues.

As for our pupils, I believe that the commitment and care they showed in their writing, and the fact that they were writing for a real audience, resulted in their own feelings of success with the project. Let us leave the last word to one of the girls, Michelle:

> I really enjoyed the lessons and the visit to G—— . . . I hope the message may have got through to the kids about sexism.

# CHAPTER 7

# Mothers and Mother-Tongue Stories

## LIZ FORSYTH

*For many parents, schools can be daunting to visit. Women from ethnic minority groups, for whom English may not be their first language, feel especially vulnerable. This chapter illustrates the mutual benefit to the teachers, children and mothers it describes, of using stories in mother tongue in the classroom. Apart from the heightened self-esteem achieved by the mothers telling the stories and the consequentially greater respect accorded them by their children, the value of bilingualism itself is underlined.*

I am a support teacher working with bilingual children in a first school where the children are between five and eight years old. I offer the classteacher various styles of support in the classroom, from focusing on one child in a group to supporting the whole class, working towards a situation where our roles are interchangeable. I also offer support to teachers across the curriculum, designing and making resources and helping forge links between home and school. Recently I have been fortunate to have an opportunity of working with the parents in our school, because the Community Education Office in our area became aware of the growing need to involve parents whose first language was not English, into the educational system of this country and for them to be involved in the process of educating their own children.

The parents (all mothers) were invited into our school for one afternoon every week to join a *milan* group. *Milan* means 'meeting' in Punjabi. At the *milan* group there were educational toys, construction kits, jigsaw puzzles, paper, crayons, etc., for the preschool children to play with their mothers, and tea was provided. Some mothers were given the opportunity to learn English through the Slough Industrial Language Centre. Classes were run for the mothers, in the school, with a crèche provided, organized on a rota basis by members of the class.

The *milan* group was very well attended. Two very enthusiastic mothers came every week to set up the room, which was the dinner hall, with tables, chairs and, of course, the tea and biscuits. Many mothers and toddlers came each week, had tea, chatted, and we had a lively, noisy group of small children playing in the hall. The English-language class, too, was well subscribed. I was very interested in the development of the group. It seemed an excellent way of having mothers in the school on their own terms. It was also a possible way for me to practise my Punjabi, which I have been learning for three years. Unfortunately, my timetabling did not allow me much time with the group. However, I did manage to squeeze in fifteen minutes each week during a TV programme as the term progressed.

I really enjoyed these fifteen minutes. I realized there was a need to impart information to the mothers, and a growing need to ask them for notices and letters to be translated. Not a week went by when I did not have a reason to go.

The mothers seemed equally pleased to see me. Although they met other members of staff in the school, they found it helpful to know that I would meet them on a regular basis every week. There was always something to talk about – either a personal worry or interest in reading books, school uniform or the Summer Fête. I began to wish I could stay with them for longer.

It was at one of these meetings that I sat next to a woman whom I had not previously met. '*As salam alekum*' ('Hello'), I said. '*Wale kum salam*' ('Greetings') she replied. '*Me tori tori Angreze bol s'k deo*' ('I do speak a little English'). I had to agree that her English was better than my Punjabi and so we continued our conversation in English.

We talked about the difficulties in learning each other's language and about our children. I was surprised when she said: 'My children are ashamed of me because of my poor English.' I asked her to explain further.

She told me that one of her children was at university and the other was studying for her A levels at a local grammar school. Throughout their education in Britain she had been unable to help them in their studies because she had not understood the language. Her husband, who had lived in England much longer than she, had been much more involved and she felt that she had been excluded from the family. I asked if the children could read and write in Urdu. They were unable to; furthermore, they had shown neither interest in nor respect for their mother tongue. Their mother's (and father's!) language was of no use to them in their high level of academic achievement.

I was interested to hear a radio programme recently concerning bilingualism in England. Assuming that it would be concerned with the languages of immigrant minorities I listened with some interest. It was indeed interesting but I was surprised to hear that the Gaelic, Cornish and Welsh languages were described as the languages of our 'forefathers'. The programme was about the 'white' ethnic languages which still exist in Britain today. Are 'white' languages given the status of belonging to our fathers and 'black' languages no status because they belong to our mothers?

If schools were to give a place to 'mother tongue' I wondered if the situation would have been any different; was the Urdu mother's story similar to that of other mothers?

When I asked her how she would have felt if Urdu had been offered to her children as a school subject she was visibly pleased and said: 'They could have learned so much from me about my culture'. I asked if she had read stories to them in Urdu, but she said they had only wanted to hear, speak and read in English. I asked if she would like to come and read stories in Urdu in our school, and she said she would be very pleased.

It was at this time that I became aware of the different role of a mother if she could not communicate well in the language in which her children were growing up. I can recall children telling me, when asked if their mothers could come to school or with us on a trip: 'No! She can't because she doesn't speak English. But my dad can!' I am aware that boys, in particular, talk positively about their fathers at work and at home but use negative tones to talk about their mothers: '*She* doesn't go out. *She* can't read this letter.'

Many parents are multilingual but our children give more status to the English that they hear, speak and read in school. We call their first language their 'mother tongue' and in schools we promote their second language. For many of us it is, of course, the only language that we speak, it is the language of Britain and children must learn to function in it to survive and to achieve in our educational system. But since the majority of countries in the world are bilingual and their bilingualism is given status, we, as teachers, ought to learn to recognize the potential of our emerging bilinguals and give equal status to both the children's 'mother tongue' and their second language. By not doing so we are preventing them from reaching their potential (as outlined in the Education Act 1944) and we are in danger of devaluing their first language, the language of their mothers.

At this particular time we were fortunate to have a new head in the Language Service of which I am part. She had recently been involved in a 'parents in partnership' project at her previous school. She had been especially interested in the sharing of reading at home and school. The parents of children at her school had met once a week, at school, and worked together to make visuals for storytelling. These visuals were used either on a magnetic or felt board as the story was told. As the parents worked, the educational value of stories and the many different aspects of reading were discussed with the teachers and parents. Parents were invited into the classrooms to tell stories using the visuals that had been made.

I felt that the *milan* group in our school could be involved in this way. I knew that if we made visuals for stories, the mothers could come into the classroom and tell stories in their mother tongue using the visuals that we had made together.

Both the Community Service and the headteacher were enthusiastic and keen to help with the project and the headteacher was able to give me time to work with the *milan* group.

I was very impressed with the visuals that had already been made; pictures had been traced, photocopied, enlarged or reduced, coloured, stuck on card, laminated and had Velcro stuck on the back so that they could be used on a feltboard.

I provided my own materials and chose 'Rupa the Elephant' as a suitable story to work on. The pictures were appealing and easy to trace. It had a repetitive storyline which was suitable and desirable for emerging bilinguals and it had been translated into several Asian languages. I also like the moral of the story. Rupa is distressed because she is grey. The brown bird helps her by asking the other animals to give her some of their colours. They look so dreadful that she washes the colours off and learns to enjoy being the colour she was intended to be. I traced the pictures and had them enlarged to a suitable size and took them to the *milan* group with some coloured felt-tip pens. I asked the mothers if they

would like to help me. A few mothers came to see what I was
doing and started to colour the animals. Another mother came to
sit next to me. I asked if she would join us but she declined saying
she did not know how to do it. I showed her and gave her lots of
encouragement but my initial enthusiasm was not taken up by
the group and I was disappointed. However, the reason for their
hesitation was made clear the next week when I had finished
colouring the animals myself and had laminated and velcroed
them. I had brought a feltboard, too, and proceeded to tell the
story using the finished visuals. I could see that the mothers were
pleased and interested in the results. It was then that I explained
the use and the value of visuals like these in the classroom for
telling stories.

At this point one mother came over to me and admitted that
she had thought I was an artist and had been using the *milan*
group to do my work for me. Because she now understood the
purpose of our colouring she was pleased to help. I had brought
some pictures of people wearing Asian clothes to colour for a
project and this time, with much more enthusiasm, we coloured
saris, chunnis, shalwars and kamiz with patterns and colours
I would never have dreamt of. Skin colours were our only
problem – felt-tip pens are not suitable for realistic skin colours.
Nevertheless, the project was under way.

What had not occurred to me was the difficulty in the actual
craft of storytelling. As teachers, we know that the most successful way is to tell stories that we know intimately, telling them as
opposed to reading them. The use of visuals enhances this technique only if the storyline is suitable. No mothers felt confident
enough to tell the Rupa story. I realized that, to have mothers
participate in the activity of storytelling, I would have to identify
a story that they knew. I was fortunate to find a mother whose
daughter did have a favourite story. It was called 'Moon Lake'.
We located it and made appropriate visuals. As we coloured
them, we talked about the story and the possibility of telling it in
Punjabi in the classroom.

By the end of term we had quite a collection of story packs. I
decided to exhibit them, not only to show the *milan* group the
extent of their work but also to show the teachers the value of
mother-tongue storytelling with attractive visuals. The exhibi-
tion was successful but the mother who was to tell 'Moon Lake'
announced that she was moving away from the area and could

no longer attend our *milan* group. I was bitterly disappointed.

As the next term began the *milan* group was much more aware of the visual-making sessions. One mother in the group, who was bilingual in Urdu and English, told me about the stories her husband told to her children and agreed to write them out for us. Once we made visuals for the first story, about a cat and a mouse, I asked her to tell the story in Punjabi in her son's classroom. I then invited the classteacher to the *milan* group so that she could welcome the storyteller into the classroom. Unfortunately, a day was chosen for the storytelling when I was not at school, the visuals could not be found and the story was told without them. The session was a disaster because, without visual stimuli, the children were inattentive and distracted. The mother was discouraged and reluctant to try again.

It had not occurred to me until this time that using visuals to tell a story was so essential. I brought the visuals and feltboard to the next *milan* group and one pre-school child was so delighted with the story that, having heard it in English, she immediately retold it in its entirety to the mothers in Punjabi, using the visuals. They could immediately see the advantage of the visuals. A mother told the story again with enormous success and enjoyment on both sides. The use of visuals in the classroom lent mother-tongue storytelling status in the eyes of the children, who realized that their mother tongue was not just for home and English for school. Without the visuals, the children felt uncomfortable and laughed, not knowing how their monolingual peers and teachers would react. Of course without them there was also no way of understanding the story if the language was not known, whereas the use of the visuals made sense of the story for *all* the children.

The mother who told the story was amazed at how much the children enjoyed the story – even more in Punjabi than English, she felt, because for many of the children it is, at six years old, the language in which they function best. They wanted to know when she would come into the classroom to do it again.

Fortunately, she had written another story, 'The Boy who Cried Wolf'. Once we had completed the visuals, she told it to the class, again in Punjabi. She was more relaxed and confident the second time and consequently she, the teacher and the children enjoyed it more.

Other mothers are now willing to take the visuals into their children's classrooms and tell the stories in their own mother tongue. We hope to continue to build up our resources and to encourage more mothers to bring their mother tongues into school.

I do believe that in order to preserve our children's bilingualism and their culture, it is our responsibility to respect and understand the role of our children's mothers and the status of their language. I have found that although I enthusiastically encourage the children to be bilingual, without a whole-school policy and realistic approval from each classteacher, most children will abandon their first language at the school gate.

I talked recently at a parents' evening with a mother who was deeply concerned that her son would not speak Punjabi at home. She and the others in her family are multilingual but her son was choosing only to speak English. I happened to be working in the class, which was in reception, and I chose to play a Punjabi recording of a well-known story. Two or three boys laughed and giggled with embarrassment throughout the story while the girls listened with obvious interest. When the story was replayed in English no one laughed. We talked afterwards about both languages and asked what the words in Punjabi meant. Only the girls answered. The children, the classteacher and I talked about how clever people are who can speak more than one language and the classteacher asked us to teach her to count in Punjabi with the children's help. Our bilingual teacher told me that not long after, the boy who was not speaking Punjabi at home came to her and told her a long story in Punjabi. One of the boys who had laughed throughout the first story in Punjabi said to me recently: 'It is very clever to speak English and Punjabi, isn't it?'

I feel that, because of our monolingual impotence, one of the best ways to encourage bilingualism is to invite our children's mothers into the classroom to share with us the responsibility of their children's education. We already welcome mothers to help with cooking and sewing, give out books in the library, and come on trips, all are undoubtedly valuable and necessary roles (though stereotypically female activities), but to share the teaching platform with us in two languages tells the children the importance we give to their home language and shows them the key role their mothers play in their learning experiences. None of the children whose mothers have come into the classroom to tell stories with the visuals ever says: 'I am ashamed of my mother.' I can only see how proud they are and how much they have enjoyed and learned from the shared experience.

Moreover the children whose mothers have come into the classroom have reacted very positively to the situation. For instance, the first mother has a son who had been very quiet in class. He showed some surprise when it was first suggested that his mother should come into school but since her visit he has become talkative, more assertive and more willing to talk to the teacher. His mother, too, feels more able to approach the teacher and talk about her concerns.

This, of course, is a project without end. It is an ongoing process. I had cause to panic slightly when our second mother was ready to go into the classroom for the first time. She was very nervous. I had asked her to tell the story in Punjabi, not realizing that she felt more comfortable speaking Urdu. When she came to the *milan* group she discussed her anxiety with her friends. As soon as I heard and understood the problem I reassured her that the children would be just as pleased to hear the story in Urdu. But she would not change because she had rehearsed the story in Punjabi. I began to realize the awesome task I had asked her to undertake.

As soon as she left the *milan* group (having looked at her watch all afternoon), her friend said: 'You shouldn't have asked her. She didn't want to do it. She'll never do it again!' I felt uncomfortable and left the classroom for the duration of the story. As the school bell went, I saw the mother coming down the corridor to meet me. 'It was wonderful!' she said. 'The children loved it. The teacher loved it, and they asked me to come again and tell another story.' I breathed a sigh of relief.

I spoke to the teacher concerned after this session. She was pleased. The children had behaved very well and she had also enjoyed the experience. She hoped that more mother-tongue stories could be told in her classroom.

I have learned a great deal from this project even though I have made many mistakes. Teachers undertaking a similar project in their schools might find the following advice helpful. They should work out exactly what they want the parents to do, when, why, with whom and how often, and discuss it with them, making sure they know what is expected of them and the rationale behind it. Once agreement has been reached, it is important for the teachers to understand that, although parents have equal interests in their children's education, they started at different points and have taken a different course. Teachers should make sure there is full co-operation and give enough time to talk and listen to parents. I think it is also important to understand that parents do have other commitments and, as teachers, we need to be flexible, helpful and reassuring and make sure they are not overstretched.

The support of the headteacher and the teachers with whom parents are expected to work is fundamental to success, as is full discussion with all colleagues about the specific aims of the project. Materials need to be made available, as do supplies of tea and coffee, but, above all, everyone involved must enjoy the opportunity of sharing and working with other equally concerned and committed adults.

## Recommended reading

Berkshire Language and Support Service (1982) *Talking and Telling*.

Croydon English Languages Scheme (n.d.) *Sharing our Languages*.

Gregory and Woolard (1984) *Looking into Language Diversity in the Classroom*, Trentham Books.

ILEA (1983) *Stories in the Multi-lingual Primary Classroom*.

Miller, Jane (1983) *Many voices, bilingualism, culture and education*, RKP.

Peterborough Centre for Multicultural Education (1984) *Language Across the Curriculum in the Multi-Cultural Primary School*.

# CHAPTER 8

# Tom, Dick and/or Harriet: Some Interventionist Strategies Against Boys' Sexist Behaviour

## ANNIE CAMPBELL AND NICOLA BROOKER

*Deliberately provocative displays of blatantly sexist behaviour by boys of primary school age are not at all uncommon. Some positive approaches in combating this problem are suggested here.*

The school we were working in is a combined church school in the centre of a very busy town. It is a modern building, all breeze-blocks and windows, designed for open plan and surrounded by a large playing field. The pupil intake is very mixed, with a large number of Urdu- and Punjabi-speaking children, as well as families from various parts of the British Isles; in fact the kind of representative cross-section of families that one might expect in an inner-city school. It also serves a fairly mobile population with a variety of family types including several single-parent families, some of whom come from local women's refuges and have understandably unsettled futures.

The subject of this chapter was a class of 10–11-year-olds in their penultimate year at the school, taught by Annie Campbell. Nicola Brooker joined them when she was assigned to the school by the Language Service to give extra support. The class consisted of equal numbers of boys and girls. The children had 'travelled' through the school together, many with relatives preceding them. Some had been together since attending the adjoining nursery school, and quite a strong permanent nucleus had formed. They had all become accustomed to one another, but if on the surface there appeared to be a general acceptance, the reality was that the class was strongly divided along gender lines, to the extent that the situation had become boys *versus* girls.

The boys tended to operate as a body under the leadership of Virnar and their behaviour and attitude affected every part of their school day. For instance, during gym lessons a 'treat' was the game 'Pirates', a game of elimination tag when the children chase each other over the apparatus without touching the floor. Depending on the boys' mood the whole game could be reduced to a sham, when no players were 'out' at all due to the boys' refusal either to touch the girls or to acknowledge their touch. In that case the whole class stayed 'in' for the entire game or all the girls would be 'out' in the first few seconds, so that the boys could enjoy complete freedom on the apparatus with the girls as bystanders. Another example during outdoor games: a boy would feign a sprained ankle rather than be beaten at the finishing line by a girl. The boys would make bargains among themselves as to who should and would win races. At dinner time, rather than queue in front of or behind any of the girls, the boys would dawdle or go to the lavatory (unnecessarily), even risking missing a decent choice of food.

Rehearsals for the class Christmas production were often brought to a standstill by Virnar's disruptive behaviour, because he felt he was entitled to the role of Father Christmas. It was not even the major role, but it was given to the most appropriate person, who was a girl. She fitted the part (and the costume fitted her!).

This antagonism and rivalry manifested itself in the classroom with verbal and physical bullying. The boys supported one another's work rather than recognizing the girls' achievements. This took the form of interrupting when the girls were speaking, not listening when the girls were reading out their work, making disruptive and personal remarks and negative comments. They would move their chairs noisily and use threatening body language, look 'daggers', wave clenched fists, pull gruesome faces and make other hostile gestures. They even went to such extremes as refusing to use a pencil-sharpener because it had just been used by a girl, and even the threat of losing 'break time' made no difference to their behaviour. The same happened with other classroom equipment such as rubbers, rulers and paper. One particular boy, Bobby, frequently disrupted the class by his refusal to sit on any chair previously used or touched by a girl or a female member of staff. The girls as a group appeared more open-minded, mature, sensitive and receptive to ideas than the boys. Their eagerness to learn did not appear to be thwarted by the boys' behaviour which they reluctantly accepted with knowing resignation, though it may have had a deeper, longer-term impact in terms of their self-perception and ultimately in their future educational choices.

This may be a scenario familiar to many teachers, though probably a more extreme manifestation of sexist attitudes. The reasons for the boys' desperate need to dominate the class and convince themselves and everyone else of their superiority can at best be speculated upon: were such factors at work as habits formed lower down the school, the influence of the school organization and structure, the composition and hierarchy of the staff, the general ethos of the school, and the presence of certain personalities within the class? Certainly equal opportunities, though recognized by individuals, were not formally discussed by the staff as a whole. Factors outside the school may also have contributed to the boys' sexism, such as family life and friendship groups.

Undoubtedly the onset of puberty contributed to the prevailing attitudes. We also feel that the imminence of the '12-plus' exam (due to be taken the next year) cannot be overlooked. This exerted a tremendous pressure on the children both at home and at school, particularly on boys who, as well as dreading failure, also found the possibility of girls passing, if they did not, very threatening.

Whatever the causes, these patterns of behaviour revealed themselves as habits that affected all classroom activities and were a main feature of every school day. Clearly the situation had to be tackled.

We adopted a variety of tactics to counteract the misery caused by the antagonism. As far as classroom organization was concerned, we made sure that the pupils sat at mixed tables. We also put a lot of emphasis on the importance of speaking out in class, giving everyone a chance to have their say, in spite of intimidation from certain boys. In particular, we encouraged the girls to speak out loudly, which did help to give them more confidence. When organizing groups to work together, we made sure that the groups were mixed and that they crossed friendship lines. All of this sounds obvious but it required constant vigilance, which could be very draining.

Discussion in the classroom has always been a central feature of our approach. The problem of the gender divide was not swept under the carpet but was openly acknowledged by us and dealt with as situations arose. One of the negative results of such frankness was that when the boys were challenged, their wish to dominate became even more urgent. We feel that the importance of humour in the defusing of these confrontations cannot be overestimated. The use of humour rather than humiliation was the tactic which helped to show up the ridiculous side of the 'laws' being imposed by the boys. Also physical contact with both boys and girls seemed to work: a slight touch on the shoulder as they were reading aloud, or holding the paper with them, gradually broke down barriers and led to confidence in speaking in front of the class and during school assemblies. Making them feel that their ideas and work were worth listening to helped them establish themselves as individuals. This in turn led to the weakening of the separate group mentality with which the boys protected themselves, and a more united class spirit emerged.

In the games lessons Annie took on a rather forceful role by choosing the teams herself. This created a better balance in that the teams were mixed in gender and ability, thus more enjoyable lessons followed with the girls being able to take a more equal part and, indeed, to shine. After initial objections the children learned to adopt this procedure themselves with less prompting from her. Another point for consideration are her own circumstances, as a female teacher, a mother with children of similar ages to the children in the class, and a single parent. These were situations with which the children could identify and which led to all sorts of unspoken understandings on all sides.

Did any part of their domestic life affect their attitude or behaviour at school? Approaching this light-heartedly and without prying was important. It was surprising to discover that many of the boys freely admitted to helping with a large number of domestic chores. They suffered no class criticism for this admission, and the most obvious reason for this seemed to be that it was done for their mothers. Once this came to light, even the 'toughest' boys took great pride in demonstrating their capabilities by taking on the cleaning jobs around the classroom. But even then their attitude that 'boys can do anything better than girls' somewhat tarnished their much appreciated efforts.

Having discussed the progress that had been achieved by the measures described above, we decided to invite the equal opportunities advisory teacher to visit, and then to carry on by planning lessons for the one afternoon a week when the three of us would be working as a team. We chose areas such as current affairs, working and domestic experiences and familiar media topics, using as many positive images of people as possible. This account of some of the lessons illustrates the sort of difficulties we encountered and examines some of our successes.

Each child developed their own folder entitled 'Heroes and Heroines' through art activities which in this class proved to be the most important and successful trigger of creative writing and self-expression.

When the children were asked 'What makes heroes and heroines?', this was the outcome:

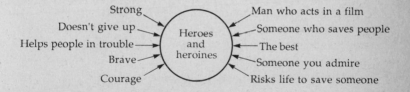

As discussion of this theme continued in the following weeks, it drew constantly on the children's opinions and experiences particularly of their families and members of different generations, and concluded with the realization that different people admire different qualities. This was a useful start because qualities in each sex which the boys were not prepared to recognize were what we hoped to continue to emphasize throughout the lessons.

For instance, after posing the question 'Are there local heroes we don't know about?' and examining qualities we admire in people, several girls came forward with thoughtful contributions. In one small group of more assertive girls, the leading light was Daisy. She had a mature attitude, was articulate and

confident, with a quiet strength of character and a good sense
of humour which meant she was not easily intimidated by
Virnar, whom she academically outstripped. Her contribution
was that heroes and heroines 'have physical and emotional
strength'. One very quiet girl volunteered 'heroes and heroines
are reliable', and a more lively one said 'heroines aren't always
pretty'.

When it was suggested that an interesting way to continue this
theme would be to interview the staff, it was predictable that all
the girls offered to take part, but only three boys.

The work of the girls developed in leaps and bounds through
their mutual support. One girl, Zahida (Father Christmas) had
been forced to adopt a more aggressive approach. Hitherto she
had endured constant jibing and harassment from all the boys,
especially Virnar. Zahida often provoked the boys but always
retaliated – if necessary, physically. The solidarity among the
girls resulted in Zahida becoming less of a 'scapegoat'; she was
enabled to participate more effectively in class, and this helped
her to cope with and control her reactions.

As the topic evolved it seemed to make no positive impression
on certain boys. The most resistant was Bobby. He was the most
disturbing and disturbed member of the class. He was not only
the slavish ally of Virnar but created his own special brand of
anarchy. He did not appear to like anyone in particular but was
obsessed by all things military. He had an unhealthy interest in
commandos, SAS uniforms, weapons and martial arts. When a
class lesson centred on occupations and the pupils' futures he said
'I'd like to be a sniper, with a machine-gun . . . and a balaclava'
and mimed the relevant actions imitating the sound of machine-
gun fire. Noises were his speciality. Remarks such as 'I like my
teacher', from Daisy, were met with facial contortions and loud
groans, interspersed with 'raspberry blowing'.

He felt he impressed the boys by calling the girls 'poofters',
'dogs', 'monkeys'. This uncomprehending use of insulting language isolated him from the rest of the class, including the boys,
but he was oblivious to this. During an otherwise relaxed exercise
under the general heading 'Values', Bobby answered the question
'What item(s) (other than person(s)) would you save from a
burning house?' with the reply: 'I would save my survival kit,
commando books and weights for fitness training.' In marked
contrast to this, Imran's short revealing answer was 'the Holy

Koran'. Imran was Virnar's closest friend in and out of school, and shared many of his attitudes towards the girls. However, through this work, in which he showed great interest and pride, he began to reveal his more refined and thoughtful characteristics. At Christmas, he unquestioningly accepted the part of a clown, which entailed dressing up in a fancy costume and a woman's wig. Undeterred by Virnar's disapproval he willingly 'danced' with a group of girls on stage. Perhaps he had the farsightedness to recognize that one outcome of this kind of activity could be more fun in the classroom. Imran was not ashamed to reveal his more sensitive and caring side, and his enthusiasm for work overcame his original loyalties to the boys and their withering dominance of the girls.

In a series of lessons we looked at the lives and careers of some women who haved achieved unusual success. Marie Curie and Florence Nightingale are among the best known of them and frequently studied by children in school. We decided to concentrate particularly on Mary Seacole, a black woman who had a prominent role as a nurse in the Crimea but whose achievements have been largely neglected. We reproduce Imran's essay on Mary Seacole. He gave an account of her life from her upbringing in Jamaica to her heroic work nursing in the Crimea.

*Mrs Seacole*
Hello are you *the* Mary Seacole? Yes I am. Could you tell me your life story? Yes of course. Well, then I was 17 and my sister was 19. We opened a hotel, well not a hotel but a kind of hospital. When I was small I was very keen to cure and help people in need as well as the people who were sick. They came to us, I was messing about with medicine I made a cure for cholera then I went to Panama because people were going there because of the gold rush and they killed themselves too. I worked there then I went for a holiday in Cuba. People were fighting and wounding each other for greed. I did work there and then I went to my home town Kingston Jamaica. I heard about the Crimean War I sold all my belongings and went to London. I went to the war officers in London I showed them all my qualifications. I was very excited but then they said NO! I was so *ANGRY* and upset but inside my mind I still had an idea. I went there myself I went through the war zone. I bought a hotel there but I made it into a hospital. I helped people there with Florence. The condition were bad, dust was everywhere. When the war stopped I got some medal and here I am!

One of the reasons for the success of this lesson was that it was a historical topic and regarded as a 'story'. However, the introduction of Dr Pauline Cutting's work in Beirut as a modern-day equivalent was received with hostility by Virnar who commented: 'So what, I could do that' and 'More fool her'.

His remarks were greeted in an uneasy silence, but none of the children was willing to tackle him. It seemed counterproductive for one of the adults to be constantly confronting him, even when he was being so blatantly provocative. However, the children looked thoughtful and worried and we were able to take up Virnar's comments later with smaller groups who felt able in this way to challenge his negative attitude.

By using many such illustrations to emphasize non-stereotypical attributes in both sexes we hope that to some extent we broke down the prevailing male ethos subscribed to by most of the boys at the start. They believed that men should be tough, that girls were inferior. Virnar even said at one stage: 'All women are wimps . . . except my mother.' Extreme remarks like this gradually came to be seen as ridiculous and lost credibility for their perpetrators. When the petty antics and trivializing behaviour of the boys became unacceptable to the class as a whole, their leadership floundered and the weaker ones realized that the continuation of hostilities only reduced school to a boring battle. As the weeks passed many realized that school, even with girls, could be fun!

We both left the school at the end of the summer term and the class went up for its last year at that school. Questions were left hanging in the air: did the children grasp the implications of our initiatives for themselves, or for us, or for the outside world? What had we achieved by exposing and then challenging certain values and beliefs? Would anyone else continue the work we had begun?

We felt that the new awareness that had slowly developed needed constant nurturing, not only academically, but in school life in general: the playground, dining-hall, greetings in the mornings, dismissals in the afternoons. The children had begun to take more pleasure in the successes and achievement of any member of the class, in and out of school, regardless of gender. Talking about success in any field and giving congratulations helped to make the peer-group bond stronger. For this progress to continue the next teacher would have to be interested in carrying on the work already begun. Brent LEA (1985a) and ILEA (1986) have been pioneers in developing and publishing whole-school initiatives. In order for similar necessary longer-lasting success to be achieved at the kind of school we have described in this chapter, a whole-staff recognition and approach to sexist attitudes is vital. We feel that our experiences bring into focus the importance of the entire school understanding and taking on the issue of equal opportunities.

## Recommended reading

Askew, Sue and Ross, Carol (1988) *Boys Don't Cry*, Open University Press.
Askew, Sue and Ross, Carol (1985) *Anti-Sexist Work with Boys*, ILEA.

# CHAPTER 9

# Towards a Non-Sexist Primary Classroom

## SUE D'ARCY

*We know that children respond to stereotypical gender expectations by the age of three and even earlier. Their first experience of school should, therefore, be used as an opportunity to begin to challenge and change sexist attitudes.*

Socialization and sex stereotyping influence and determine children's characters and attitudes from birth. Home, media and nursery will all have greatly affected a child before she/he enters the school premises and sexist views may already be firmly established. It is essential that teachers are aware of this so that in their teaching they can educate children to examine, discuss and reject stereotypes. Power in Britain is deliberately engineered to ensure an unequal and sexist society. Unless schools make conscious efforts to intervene they inevitably perpetuate the assumptions underlying this inequality. This patently unjust situation can only begin to be eliminated by tackling the problem of sexism at the earliest stage of a child's development: hence the importance of the non-sexist primary classroom.

Both girls and boys are victims of sexism in that girls learn that they are expected to be caring, loving and gentle in preparation for motherhood, while boys are forbidden to show emotion, especially fear or sadness. It is therefore vital for teachers to examine and question their relationships with their pupils and also the classroom environment that they create.

I will be drawing on experiences and situations encountered during my teaching of two reception classes and two lower junior classes in both a multi-ethnic school and a school where the intake is mainly white middle-class. I have always been

committed to anti-racism and anti-sexism and these are both
reflected in my teaching and the classroom environment I create.
I have tried to ensure that this chapter focuses on the practical
rather than the theoretical as it is through personal experiences
that we can often realize the effect of actions and situations and
thus learn from them.

## The classroom environment

Children learn best in an atmosphere which is happy and relaxed,
encouraging their individual freedom of thought and development. The classroom atmosphere is fundamental to children
developing their own individuality, forming their own opinions
and satisfying their innate curiosity. They need to experience a
variety of learning strategies. These will range from tightly structured activities to open-ended situations which will encourage
detailed intellectual discussion and will allow them to voice their
views and draw their own conclusions.

Teachers create and control the atmosphere in their classrooms
through actions, expressions, words and voice, and children
respond to all of these continually. They should never under-
estimate their importance and effect on their pupils. Confidence
and trust are fundamental to learning – children do need to feel
this in their relations with teachers and peers if they are to participate in activities and discussions which may raise sensitive issues
and evoke powerful emotions.

## Organizational strategies

The physical classroom environment and its organization obviously influence the children in their interactions and studies. I
always aim to organize the children to work together in mixed
groups. If this is begun as soon as children enter school and
continued throughout, they are less likely to develop antagonistic
attitudes which can completely disrupt and ruin a good working
classroom environment. I have, for instance, seen 11-year-old
boys refusing to sit on chairs because they had formerly been
occupied by girls and once witnessed a boy violently jabbing at a
girl's book with his ruler because he refused to touch any of her

belongings and her property was on his side of the table. We need to foster caring physical relationships in all children, especially in boys, in order to help them channel and express their affections and feelings.

Lining up was a problem which I found much simpler to resolve with five-year-olds than eight-year-olds. In my reception classroom I asked the children to find a partner of the opposite sex and to line up with that person. This ensures physical contact between girls and boys which is valuable in fostering considerate behaviour. They complied with hardly a murmur and continued this behaviour, with an occasional reminder, throughout the year. Junior-aged children provided more resistance because of their already established school routine and hardened perspectives on gender as they grew older. The children refused to line up with a partner of the opposite sex, so after much deliberation I asked them to line up in two lines – one line consisting of children whose surnames began with letters from the first part of the alphabet, A–L, the second line formed of children whose surnames began with M–Z. Admittedly, when the children walked around school their opposite in line was not always of the opposite sex, but the children were not strictly segregated by sex. Initially, they had to concentrate to make sure they stood in the correct line and therefore were too preoccupied to manipulate who their partners were going to be. It also, incidentally, provided an alternative method of learning the alphabet!

Registration used to raise problems in that I felt it was unfair that the boys were always listed first, giving them an unjustified sense of importance and superiority. I discussed the issue with the headteacher and the school secretary and on discovering that there was no specific reason for listing by gender, we decided, as school policy, to list the children in strict alphabetical order, regardless of sex. This came as a complete surprise to the children who were fascinated to know why the registration order had changed, and proved a very valuable basis for discussion of equality. The children agreed that the old system was completely unfair and outmoded, and were unanimously in support of the new method.

## Organization of classroom areas

It is also important that the areas in a classroom should be closely monitored to ensure that they do not become predominantly a male or female domain. A science or CDT area may attract more boys and thus become male-orientated. From observations in my own classroom I have found that girls become reticent because they have to fight for the equipment they need, the boys tending to expect to carry out all the exciting manipulative and experimental work. The resulting constant friction makes for a bad-tempered atmosphere, wearing for both pupils and teachers. In these circumstances it can be tempting to capitulate to the boys. Boys will often ignore girls and their contributions, even very valuable ones, and girls have less confidence because they have often had fewer opportunities in working with construction equipment. Yet these same girls are usually more adept than their male counterparts at fastening buttons, buckles, and so on – skills which require the same degree of fine touch. It would appear that boys have little incentive to learn these skills because they are not demanded of them at home (Belotti, 1975). Girls need to recognize the advantages of transferring this facility to science and CDT.

In an effort to combat this, I encouraged girls to work together in single-sex groups in specific classroom areas to try to ensure they had time to experiment and gain confidence. This procedure continued for over a term and was successful for many girls. They became more assertive in challenging the boys' automatic assumption that they had first refusal over classroom equipment. The boys also recognized changes in the girls' attitude to the extent of asking for their help.

The play area or play house is a largely female domain and children often assume stereotypical roles on entering it. Girls are pleased to act out stories and situations. However, boys seem unhappy in deferring to the girls in this context and I have often observed boys changing roles to become animals, introducing elements of aggression, noise and disruption to the situation. I recorded a group of children playing in the clothes shop:

Fahmida and Puja are playing happily in role in the shop.
Graham and Joseph decide to be dogs.

*Graham*: I'm a guard dog.
*Joseph*: Please be a monster.

*Graham*: No, I'm a guard dog.
*Fahmida*: I'm a monster.
*Puja*: I'm a lion.
*Puja*: I'm a sister dog.
*Joseph*: Pretend we're friends.

   Fahmida in the shop is beginning to be genuinely scared of the screams and other noises.

   Puja puts her 'paw' up and strokes her.

   Fahmida also becomes a lion.

   Fahmida is anxious to please Joseph and thus offers to be a monster. The situation gets very noisy and Puja realises Fahmida's fears and immediately goes to comfort and reassure her. She restores calm to the group.

This example illustrates the difficulties Graham and Joseph experience in adapting to this kind of role play. Instead they disrupt and subvert it. When their play becomes fraught it rests with a girl to redeem the situation.

   I felt that providing a house or home-corner for the children to play in in isolation did not provide enough challenges and so I decided to link the play area with the class topic. Thus, the area becomes on occasion a veterinary surgery (Animal topic), a café (Food topic) or a shop (Local Environment topic) – the possibilities are endless! Children still have the very valuable learning experiences of 'house play' but can assume a wider variety of characters which enriches their imagination and play.

## Physical contact and relationships in the classroom

Interaction between teachers and pupils consciously needs to be addressed. As research has shown, boys demand more attention than girls (see, for example, Spender, 1982) and it seems sometimes almost impossible to rectify the situation. It is nevertheless our duty to try to redress the balance. Perhaps we are half-way there when we can recognize what is happening, remembering that patterns for black girls are different (Wright, 1987). However, combating the male domination of classrooms is a different matter. One of my solutions was to try to ignore any interruptions for as long as possible but this is certainly not ideal and often cannot be achieved. I did devise some strategies which included gently touching the disruptive children, putting their hand down or placing a finger on their or my lips. I would also try and use positive reinforcement: 'Yasir is sitting really quietly and has his hand up' but sometimes had to resort to: 'I'm not going to ask anyone who shouts out'.

Physical contact between teacher and pupil and between pupils themselves is very important. I have tried to foster in my children consideration and a sense of responsibility for one another. I have spent time discussing situations which have upset the children to prove to them that I care and also to help them all recognize that we as individuals can be influential in determining to a greater or lesser extent another person's happiness and sense of well-being. Topics such as 'friendship', 'name calling', and 'anger' can become almost daily discussion points and can be depressing for the teacher, but incidents must be dealt with immediately, whenever possible. It is perfectly acceptable for the teacher to let children see her/his unhappiness at their behaviour – if a close teacher–pupil relationship has been built up, this will be significant to the children.

Encouraging and giving children the confidence to talk about or in some cases simply to admit to certain emotions and feelings is a major step in learning to care. In the reception class the majority of boys could not at first admit to crying if they were hurt physically or emotionally. Vineet and Sanjeev are twin brothers who had very clearly defined views on acceptable behaviour for boys. Vineet recounted a story about getting his finger stuck in a door. He concluded:

> *Vineet*: I didn't cry, but Sanjeev did.
> *Sanjeev*: I didn't! I didn't cry!
> *Vineet*: Yes you did!
> *SD*: If you saw that your brother was hurt you would have been upset. Everyone cries when they're upset – mummies, daddies, aunties, uncles. I cry when I'm hurt or very sad. It's OK to cry. (*Sanjeev nods uncertainly.*)

I spent many hours talking about experiences, real and imaginary, with the children and role-playing familiar playground and classroom incidents. 'Gently' was a word I wanted them to internalize and reflect in their behaviour and I feel I achieved this by being gentle and concerned myself and encouraging the children to perform tasks 'gently' or look after each other 'gently'. By the end of the school year children could freely admit that they cried and were not embarrassed or ashamed. The value of this cannot be overemphasized as I strongly believe that many people, especially men, find difficulty in expressing their feelings and emotions as a result of continually suppressing them.

Another major factor I want to include is the influence of disabled children. One of my pupils is a girl who is virtually blind. She can only see large blocks of colour. Physically she is tiny and frail and this, combined with her disability, fostered surprisingly solicitous behaviour in all the other children. The child, whom I shall call Aisha, appeared almost ungendered when she came to school – she did not seem to notice the 'difference' between boys and girls. She was always conscious of what she was wearing – focusing on colour and texture rather than her overall appearance. As a Muslim she had to cover her legs but was unconcerned whether the clothes she wore consisted of Western-style trousers and jumper or pretty feminine shalwar kamiz. However, even she is now changing, influenced by school and the media.

Aisha had a very calming effect on her peers, and her influence allowed the boys to adopt female roles with greater ease. For example, Dino was conscious of his masculinity and was often extremely disruptive and aggressive. This, however, is how he behaved with Aisha:

> *Dino*: I'm the mum. (*Puts on white dress and gets a handbag to put money in.*)
> *Aisha*: I'm the baby. (*Gets in pram.*)

> Dino pushes the pram out of the shop and gently takes Aisha for a walk. More remarkably, Dino then climbs into the pram himself and allows Aisha to push him, saying 'I'm her baby.'

Aisha thus encouraged a more protective attitude in Dino, and allowed him to take on a role he would usually find difficulty in relating to. It is commonly assumed that disabled children *cause* problems in a classroom. As we can see, Aisha helps to *mitigate* the problems fuelled by Dino's aggression.

The children were also keen to take responsibility in an unpatronising way for Aisha and when working or playing with her, displayed mature behaviour often lacking in their relationships with others. This was excellent experience for the children but did not help Aisha's independence – the children then had to learn to let Aisha explore for herself but be prepared to intervene if needed, which is surely excellent preparation for adulthood and parental responsibility.

## Language

While language is fundamental to all learning, all communication and all aspects of social life, it is, unfortunately, easy to use stereotyped clichés even inadvertently and as teachers we must try to be constantly aware of this. It often seems simpler to reinforce stereotypes than to eradicate them, especially as they are portrayed in so many posters, books, television programmes, games and puzzles.

## Resources

With the limited resources one has in a classroom, the lack of money, not to mention the noticeable absence from the market of material which is positively and realistically presented, one has to use and adapt what is available. There are many wonderful stories which do nevertheless contain strong gender stereotypes in the text or illustrations. These I feel can still be valuable, imaginative or adventurous experiences for children. It would not be fair or right to remove them from the classroom but it is essential to provoke discussion enabling children to learn to identify stereotypes and to question and reject them. They need to recognize that many 'book families' are completely outdated, historically located, and totally unfamiliar to their lives.

Quite often I have found that posters and books which are non-sexist or anti-racist are cheaply made, have black and white illustrations and are poorly presented. Of course this is due to a lack of financial backing but it does mean the children find them less appealing, take less care with them and are less affected by them. I felt very concerned by the lack of choice of non-sexist stories and approached a local secondary school to see if a project could be set up in which teenagers could write stories for the children in their local infant school as part of their English GCSE course. This was accomplished and, judging by the children's obvious delight and enjoyment, was very successful (see Chapter 6).

## Reading

Fiction is powerful in all our lives and children are no exception to this. Stories can fire imaginations and provide a basis for role-playing. Children become totally absorbed in their imaginary situations, which often seem real to them. If we feel that children are susceptible to the influence of fiction then it is necessary to ensure that their reading material is as unbiased as possible from their earliest school experience.

Unfortunately, reading schemes generally do not seem to be changing with the times. Many schools still use outdated schemes. I have always used the 'Individualized Approach to Reading' devised by Cliff Moon, where books are categorized into levels of difficulty and coded by a colour – children then read widely at their own level. The children thus come into contact with a wide variety of schemes, and certain schemes, or even particular books, which are blatantly sexist or racist can be excluded. Of course, this system is expensive to install but money spent on reading material is well spent if it motivates children, fosters good reading habits and provides enjoyment.

My favourite reading scheme at the time of writing is Roderick Hunt's 'Oxford Reading Tree' which is amusing, true to life, beautifully presented and, perhaps most important of all, very appealing to children. The illustrations are realistic – Mum actually wears jeans and a sweatshirt – and comical, and the children in the stories have adventures which could happen to anyone. Mum is seen to be painting, helping to assemble a swing using a spanner and in a variety of other roles. One can always find points to criticize, but I do feel that it is a scheme which focuses on people one might meet. This does not conform to the usual stereotypes and does not hide under the umbrella of animal characters. It is worth noting that books which use animals instead of people often give them a gender by dressing the mother rabbit in an apron, for instance, or implicitly assuming that animals have inherent 'gendered' qualities, which are based on stereotypes – for example, cats are female, bears are male.

Some schools make their own reading-book material using photographs of the children themselves at school and at home. This means sexist and racist stereotypes can be eliminated but does provide an increased workload for teachers.

Perhaps the most important thing to remember is to be continually aware. I have examined schemes which I felt were acceptable yet suddenly, while sharing a book with a child, I have recognized a blatant stereotype which hitherto I had failed to notice. We have to be prepared to examine and re-examine, consider and re-consider all new schemes carefully as they are introduced.

## Music

I have always enjoyed music and singing with children I have taught, and feel it provides pleasure, a sense of togetherness and an opportunity for all to participate in the same activity regardless of ability. I remember becoming aware of the sexist lyrics in many songs and feeling angry that females were portrayed as nagging, giggling or spiteful characters in songs like 'The Wheels on the Bus Go Round and Round': 'The mums on the bus go chatter, chatter, chatter'. I decided to change lyrics which offended me. This was not as time-consuming as I expected, and made me feel much happier in that children were singing about and internalizing positive images. Many songs are centred on children who perform a certain action or activity. One such song is 'Five Currant Buns in a Baker's Shop' (see Matterson, 1969). Every verse includes the line 'Along comes a boy with a penny one day', and I have watched a number of teachers choosing one boy after another to perform the actions while the expressions on the girls' faces varied from disappointment to anger. Substituting 'Along came a child' or alternating between girls and boys solves the problem immediately.

I include examples of two popular songs which I altered to show how easy it is to do.

### The families on the bus go off to town

The families on the bus go off to town, off to town, off to town,
The families on the bus go off to town, off to town.
The mums on the bus buy the tickets, tickets, tickets . . .
The girls on the bus hold the money, money, money . . .
The dads on the bus hold the shopping, shopping, shopping . . .
The boys on the bus hold the tickets, tickets, tickets . . .
The aunties on the bus read the paper, paper, paper . . .
The uncles on the bus look after the babies, babies, babies . . .
The bell on the bus goes ding a-ling, a-ling . . . [1]

### Majid was a cook and this is what he did

Majid was a cook, and this is what he did:
– He put on his check trousers,

– What did he do then?
– He put on his clean apron,
– What did he do then?
– He put his big white hat on,
– What did he do then?
– He made a cake for us to eat,
– Yum, yum, yum, yum,
– That's what he did then.

Della was a fire lady and this is what she did:
– She put on her boots and leggings,
– She put on her yellow jacket,
– She put her fire lady's hat on,
– She jumped into the engine,
– Cling, clang, cling, clang.

Mandeep was a nurse and this is what he did:
– He put on his white jacket,
– He put his shiny badge on,
– He put his nurse's watch on,
– He made the bed all nice and neat,
– Tuck, tuck, tuck, tuck.[2]

Some songs are not so easy to alter and I would rather not use them. 'Happiness is . . .' (see Gadsby and Hoggarth, 1980) is a song which gives twelve examples of what happiness is to a variety of different people and is popular with children. The examples are almost all male, as in this verse:

To a preacher it's a prayer, prayer, prayer,
To the Beatles, it's a yeah, yeah, yeah,
To a golfer it's a hole in one,
To a father, it's a brand new son.

There are only two direct references to females:

To a showgirl, it's a mink, mink, mink,

and

To my mother, well it's me, me, me!

Although the tune is appealing, I feel the images portrayed in the lyrics are too damaging – subtle sexism will not be recognized by children, especially when in the form of a song. Maximum energy and concentration will be spent in singing in tune – not in debating and pondering the words.

## Conclusion

As teachers, we need to analyse all aspects of our teaching – our approach, organization and curriculum – to enable us to recognize sexism, to ensure that we are not, even inadvertently, sexist. It is time-consuming and can seem unrewarding but the effect of teachers on their pupils is so powerful and influential that every effort must be made to present children with unbiased material. We must ensure that our whole approach is designed to break down stereotypes and provide children with the opportunity to develop as individuals in their own right.

## Notes

1 Adapted from 'The Wheels on the Bus Go Round and Round' in Harrop (1976).
2 Adapted from 'Danny Was a Cowboy', *Talkabout* (ITV), broadcast in 1986.

# CHAPTER 10

# Consultation, Persuasion, Adoption – Developing a School Policy on Gender

## DEREK TUTCHELL

*As more and more schools become convinced of the need for a whole-school policy on gender equality, various successful models are evolving. This is an account of how one primary school developed a policy over a period of time. Parents, teachers and school governors are all involved in the changes now taking place in schools. The practical ideas in this chapter can be adapted to suit individual needs in other schools.*

Of one thing I am sure – it is not an overnight accomplishment. The creation, adoption and implementation of an equal opportunities policy takes time. It has taken a long time to operate a policy for equal opportunities in the school in which I work, and many would argue that the operation is a long way from being successful yet. There were many reasons for the length of the gestation period. We were learning as we felt our way forward, we had no model to follow and, in the early days (1979–80), no guidance from advisers. Although anti-sexist work had started in schools around the country, it was still fragmented. Reading Dale Spender's (1980) book, *Man-Made Language*, was my own personal catalyst.

I imagine that teachers engage with the need for equal opportunities by responding to varied stimuli. As far as I was concerned, there was no vision on the road to Damascus but a gradual realization that the inequalities I had witnessed in education, especially in the schools in which I had taught and in which I was now a headteacher, were based on class inequalities and exacerbated by attitudes towards race and gender, compounded by teaching methods.

The impetus to do something about gender inequality came from three of the staff in the first school in which I was head-teacher. Their motivations were mixed but they were united in their determination that things should change. We were aware of the time given to behaviour problems with boys, and that girls were underachieving. My feelings then, as now, are that attitudes learnt at home are nurtured in the primary school and hardened at secondary level. However, I realized that I was in a position to encourage and promote gender equality in my own primary school, at least.

We had already spent some time talking about racial equality and had begun to devise a multi-racial educational policy with accompanying guidelines. Again this was being done without benefit of guidance or advice from the Education Office or advisers, but a number of staff were attending short courses and reading relevant material. In 1977, another Brent head and I were seconded for a term to take a course on multi-cultural education in order to firm up our school policies and finalize their guidelines, which the LEA hoped to use as models. We had started discussing a policy on gender before my secondment, if only in terms of school organization. By the time I had returned from secondment, re-established my role in the school and pro-duced and discussed our policy on multi-cultural education it was 1978, and in that year I moved to my present school, so that, ultimately, gender was not dealt with.

The new school, similar to my last but larger, is a Group 6 school with 450 on roll, a junior and infants school with a nursery class. The school is situated in a working-class area with mainly rented accommodation, and the proportion of black children was then about 50 per cent and is now about 80 per cent divided equally between Afro-Caribbean and Asian children.

When I arrived at the school in 1979 I found confirmed what I had already believed to be the case: that there was a prime need for a policy on multi-cultural education. This was to become my priority. I thought long and hard about a policy on gender but I admit not hard or long enough. On reflection, I believe we would have finally succeeded in doing both together, but at the time I considered that a staff of 23 working to a very formal curriculum with very precise record-keeping in literacy and maths were just possibly ready to be confronted with an issue which would question fundamental attitudes, which could undermine self-confidence, which would search out insecurity in some, but *not* to take on board *two* fundamental reviews of curriculum.

It is considered unwise to take over a new post and from the first day be seen to treat it as a glorious crusade or a formidable challenge. The governors and the parents may well approve, but this attitude may not be shared by the teachers. When that school sees no need for dramatic and disturbing confrontation, there is even less cause. The school was functioning perfectly well to a high level of attainment but within a very restricted and prescriptive curriculum.

A large number of the staff had been in residence for many years but there was a small nucleus of probationers who were obviously going to be good teachers but were using all their energies on learning the basics of the job. This staff, with two distinct elements, was unused to consultation, and more used to accepting prescribed guidelines and policy. I determined to follow the practice they were familiar with and present the staff with a ready made policy on multi-cultural education. Its implementation through various areas of the curriculum, however, required lengthy consultation. The methods we used became a model for the later implementation of a policy on gender equality. The material we used came from the Centre for Urban Educational Studies and concentrated on anti-racial strategies for the classroom.

While considering the policy for racial equality, it was never far from our minds that there was a need for a policy on gender equality and indeed the discussion on racial equality had emphasized that for others on the staff.

The organization of the school was determined by sexist attitudes. Everything that could be done to differentiate the sexes seemed to be done – playground lines, corridor lines, registers and all other class lists, boy monitors controlling corridors, girl monitors with infants, a far from unisex uniform, the male deputy head in charge of boys' welfare, but the head of infants for that of the girls.

There was already some awareness of the need for an anti-racist curriculum – Janet and John were long gone and the current reading scheme (the school now uses the 'real' book approach) reflected an anti-racist and anti-sexist approach. However, it was still needlework for girls and craft for boys, and fourth-year games was still football for the boys (including those who did not like it) while the girls occupied the fringe areas in unorganized games of rounders or throwing balls to one another on the sidelines. The PE and games apparatus was handled by the boys, the topic or theme work (usually on integral part of the Primary School syllabus) seemed to be for the boys, chosen by the boys and enjoyed by them.

Then, in 1981–2 came a number of catalysts. A policy on gender equality could have been and can be achieved without any of them but it certainly eased the task in the school and gave all of us a focus for our discussions. First, a new member of staff arrived who was very interested in the role of girls and women in society and education, who was an experienced teacher and who had a strong academic background. Then came the appointment by the LEA of an adviser for equal opportunities, Hazel Taylor, who within the year had organized courses which were attended by myself and the interested teachers from the school. From the people attending these courses, Hazel Taylor invited a group of primary school teachers to form a working party to produce a policy statement for the Borough of Brent and one of the teachers in our school, Kim Beat, who had shown great interest, was appointed to chair that working party (Brent, 1985a).

In the middle of 1984 we started work on a policy based on Hazel Taylor's suggested structural prerequisites: a well-established system of democratic consultation so that policy decisions are taken by the staff as a whole, mixed-ability teaching, parental and community involvement and a subject-integrated curriculum. Later that year the LEA decided that every school would be required to produce a policy on gender equality. In February 1985 all work on a policy came to a standstill because of a dispute between the unions and the employers; all goodwill was exhausted, and all out-of-school activity, which included staff curriculum development, ceased. Because of this action, discussion and consultation did not fully start again until the autumn of 1986. By then, to a large extent, the impetus had gone but a final boost was given when the LEA let it be known that every school should present its governing body with its policy in the spring term of 1987.

Discussion and consultation restarted with a 'social seminar' one evening. I had started these evenings at my previous school and they had often proved very valuable. Those members of staff who wished to, met at the home of a colleague to talk about an issue or topic prepared by one of us. The context of these meetings had been very varied – pastoral, curricular or about the organization of the school – and with people there wanting to talk and with wine and sometimes food to relax everyone, fruitful discussion took place. No minutes were ever taken and no decisions made because the meeting was 'unofficial' as not all staff could, or wanted to, be present. But the discussion generated formed a good springboard for formal full-staff debate, especially as it encouraged diffident staff to provide an input. The evening seminar allowed the first of many worries, prejudices and insecurities to be aired. We were thus able to spend a long time dealing with such matters as parental influence, upbringing, the feeling that teachers cannot change society, and so on.

A small group of committed teachers had been the backbone of these meetings on gender, but now a much larger group of interested and keen staff was recruited. I then decided to hold a full-staff session in which we would discuss what I consider to be the basis of gender equality – language. Language is the method by which we make our verbal communications; it is obviously used in textbooks and reading schemes. Everyone feels they have contributions to make about its relevance without worrying too much about the inhibiting linguistic theories. We watched a video recording of a BBC TV programme from the series *Scene*, 'Words Fail Us', which generated a long discussion on various aspects of gender and language. There were still two or three who, for various reasons, felt threatened. The sole contribution to discussion of the one who felt most affronted was 'What a load of rubbish!' which was actually quite useful because she acted as a catalyst. Her outburst did start people thinking about language and its bias in favour of '*man*kind'. This discussion was followed by co-operative activities in pairs and fours which required every member of staff to take part, exploring their own use of language and their peceptions of other people's.

The next step was a 'brainstorming' session with all the staff. Brainstorming is an informal activity in which everyone can join and, indeed, even the most reticent teachers on the staff chose to do so. In this case the topic was 'Gender Equality' and the deputy head, who chaired the meeting, noted all contributions as they were made. The blackboard suggestions were then transferred to an overhead projector classified under three headings (see below). These lists were typed out and distributed to staff before the next meeting.

## GENDER EQUALITY

| *Organization* | *Curriculum* | *Management* |
|---|---|---|
| Responsibilities | Games | Language |
| Tidying up | Drama | Emotions |
| Toilets | Reading schemes | Tidying up |
| Changing | Books | Changing |
| School uniform | TV | Playhouse |
| Behaviour – attitudes | Poetry | Behaviour – attitudes |
| Dinner ladies | Sewing | Position in class |
| Wet weather | Woodwork | Stereotypes |
| Visitors | Religion – racist | Pictures |
| Stereotypes | Parents' attitudes | Dressing-up |
| Pictures | Singing | Work Cards |
| Dressing-up | Swimming | Resources |
| Positions of authority | Playhouse | Stories |
| Non-teaching staff | Visitors | Cooking |
| New children | Stereotypes | New children |
| Careers – | Cultural backgrounds | Careers – |
|    expectations | Science |    expectations |
| Language | Pictures | Lining-up |
| Male/female staff | Maths | Apparatus |
| Emotions | Dressing-up | Crying |
| Lining-up | Work cards | Toys in classroom |
| Apparatus | Resources | Dolls |
| Medicals | Stories | TV |
| Crying | Cooking | Responsibilities |
| TV | Careers – | Manners |
| Consolation |    expectations | Jokes |
| Assemblies | Dancing | Assemblies |
| Manners | Language | Consolation |
| Jokes | | |
| Clubs – timetabling | | |
| Religions – racist | | |
| Sports kit | | |

The next step was to divide the staff into three working parties, one for each of the classifications. Before describing further procedures I must explain that, like the 'social seminar' and the 'brainstorming', the division into working parties was a

procedure with which the staff were familiar. It was a procedure
we had followed, at the deputy head's suggestion, when formu-
lating a policy for multi-cultural education. The advantages of
smaller working parties are that everybody takes part in discussion (carefully appointed chairpersons make sure of that) and
that a lot more ground can be covered. The disadvantage is that
plenary sessions can be repetitive if all the groups' discussions and
decisions are to be comprehensively understood, especially as all
decisions taken by groups had to be agreed by all the staff. However experience had taught that a minimum of talk at plenary
sessions with sufficient written material (minutes and decisions)
available beforehand ensured maximum staff participation. Its
advantages thus outweighed the disadvantages. I cannot pretend
that all the staff were enthusiastic all of the time, indeed one or
two needed persuasion to participate, but at least they could see a
structured activity in which they could play a part.

Thus the staff divided into three groups of seven or eight, the
selection of the groups covering age range of children, experience, status and interests of teachers. The deputy head was asked
to chair School Organization, the head of infants to chair
Classroom Organization and the teacher on the Borough Working Party to chair Curriculum. Groups were asked to make recommendations over the full age range of the school, and to put
these recommendations into a form that should be acceptable to
all the staff. The curriculum group were given a difficult but
challenging task – their recommendations had to cover the curriculum in general and not specific subject areas. Copies of each
group's recommendations were given to all staff before they next
met in plenary session.

It required two full sessions to discuss and approve recommendations on School Administration and Class Organization
because, despite the fact that much debate took place informally
in the staffroom and also within the groups, there were still teachers who needed convincing not of the need for gender equality
but of our capability of putting our principles into practice. At
the end of the second plenary session it was resolved *nem. con.*
that decisions on action to implement policy were binding on all
staff – and this was made clear to those who abstained.

Now we needed to discuss curricular areas: our next task was
to decide what the curricular areas should be and the composition
of the working parties. Again we were following a similar pattern

to that used in discussion on the curriculum before. It was decided to divide the staff into smaller working parties this time, five or six to a group, and again to cover the age range of the school and to take note of the status and experience of the teachers. Also this time we tried to match interests. Language, maths, science and social studies (humanities) were the first four areas dealt with and later the working parties were restructured to cover creative art, music, RE, movement and drama, PE and games. Teachers with posts of responsibility or with special interests were asked to chair the groups and I moved between groups to form an overall picture. This second round of working parties did much the same as the first: that is, they made recommendations based upon the curriculum guidelines already on file and then in plenary session these were discussed and resolved, the results of their deliberations having been circulated beforehand. The third round then discussed the second set of curriculum areas, produced recommendations, and these were discussed, approved and finalized in plenary session.

The full recommendations were produced a year ago and were received by the school governors at their spring meeting. It was agreed that discussion should take place at the summer-term meeting when they had had a chance to digest the document. The production of the document achieved a great deal and the whole process, lengthy as it was, made us not only consider gender equality but re-consider, debate and discuss anti-racist strategies and indeed the curriculum in general.

As with any other school policy, it is constantly under review, particularly with changes of personnel on the staff. There has been no doubt of the value of our work in creating a sustained awareness of gender issues as we develop and reassess our own commitment to equality of opportunity.

So we have had to ask ourselves: did we achieve Hazel Taylor's four prerequisites (p. 95)? Democratic consultation and decision certainly happened, mixed-ability teaching was already taking place, a subject-integrated curriculum was on the way. However, parental/community involvement remains at the level of governors and certainly as far as parents are concerned that is not enough. At the very least we now need to offer them our guidelines and then the opportunity to discuss, question and pronounce. And then, of course, to enact the policy and monitor it.

# CHAPTER 11

# A Joint Primary/Secondary Integrated Science Scheme

## JOHN SIRAJ-BLATCHFORD AND JEREMY LOUD

*Collaboration between primary and secondary schools is a vital element in establishing greater equality in both race and gender. Science teaching is often criticized as an area of the curriculum where greater sensitivity to these issues is needed. This experiment, involving two neighbouring schools, a combined school and a secondary school, on an anti-sexist/anti-racist science project, highlights both the positive gains and the setbacks encountered.*

At the end of the summer term of 1987 Langleywood Secondary School in Slough embarked upon a project with Foxborough, a feeder school. The project aimed to explore the potential for the promotion of anti-sexism and anti-racism in the context of primary–secondary liaison. At both schools we were concerned to address attention primarily to the underachievement in science which we felt had too often been interpreted uncritically as evidence of the low ability of students. What seemed to be crucial in this respect was the way in which pupils saw themselves as 'scientists' in the laboratory and the way in which their self-image was affected by pedagogy. It was felt that science education had for too long been separated from its applications and from students' everyday life. We did not want to see pupils merely doing 'practicals'; we wanted to see them engaged in genuine 'scientific research'. The following chapter offers an account of the project and a consideration of some of the lessons learnt.[1]

The project sought to provide opportunities for students to reappraise their attitudes to gender and racial stereotypes from within a context of energy education. Both schools were also concerned to find new ways to ease the transition from primary to secondary school. The project evaluation took the form of personal construct grids and oral interviews. We were keen to influence the practices and attitudes of colleagues by involving them as far as possible in an integrated scheme. We also felt that pupils were in need of some programme of attitude remediation to combat both sexism and racism and that a common strategy was possible. The publication of the Swann Report (Department of Education and Science, 1985)[2] reinforced these convictions and offered valuable support to our case for implementing the project. Research suggested that, at the age of 11, boys and girls were equally interested in science, albeit in different themes; boys were already 'tinkering' with machines and technology. By the end of the secondary phase girls were grossly underrepresented in the physical sciences (APU, 1986). ILEA (1983) showed that overall, girls were entered in science examinations for fewer subjects than boys but that on average girls achieved better grades than boys in all examination levels, including physics at CSE, O level and A level. As the report concluded, the problem was not, therefore, simply one of achievement but concerned the factors which influenced girls away from the subject. The report reviewed the literature in the field and considered the possible reasons for the underrepresentation, concluding that the lack of effective role models in perceived 'male' areas, the 'masculine' presentation of much of the subject matter, sexist texts, peer-group pressures and the lack of adequate option choice and careers counselling are all contributing factors.

Our initial cross-curricular integrated proposal was drawn up by a co-ordinator from each school in collaboration with colleagues. Strategies were discussed and materials developed. This work was significantly influenced by research conducted by the Children's Learning in Science Project[3] and by the Association for Curriculum Development in Science.[4] A 'process science' and 'problem-solving' approach was adopted. We hoped to provide genuine illustrations and experiences of technological problem-solving, showing a logical process interspersed with bursts of intuitive/divergent thinking. It is obviously good teaching practice to build up concepts starting from individual practical experiences. Unfortunately this is not always achieved for large groups, even in the best of laboratories and classrooms. It was felt that failure in lessons was normally due to the pupil becoming actively discouraged. The implications of failure are, however, all the more serious for girls and black pupils who may, given the dominant images and attitudes in our society, take this failure upon themselves rather than blaming the teacher or apparatus. Strategies were therefore planned and every effort made to promote the maximum success and encouragement.

The project benefited from management support and encouragement and was facilitated to some extent by the removal of key secondary staff from the 'cover list' during periods cleared by departing fifth-years. In the event the initial proposal was to be considerably tailored to fit in with other commitments of the Junior School, such as a concern to keep 'formal', separate, language and number sessions rather than relying upon full integration, and by the 'School Play', the success of which was considered heavily dependent upon the efforts of the fourth-year leavers. These priorities were considered to be of paramount importance. It also seemed that some Junior School staff lacked faith in curriculum integration. Eventually we were forced to revise our plans and settle for a total of two afternoon and two morning sessions split between the sites and covering science, computer and music work at Langleywood and science and CDT at Foxborough.

Thirty-eight fourth-year pupils alloted themselves, voluntarily, to three groups, one all-girl group, one all boys and one mixed. Most of the pupils said that they wanted to 'work with their friends'; several of the girls expressed feelings of inhibition about working with boys, with comments such as 'they get all the good ideas' or 'they usually grab all the equipment'. One of the girls suggested that 'if you're with the boys then, there, they show off a bit, they muck about too much, but with the girls they get on with it'. The boys comments were more aggressive, emphasizing 'not needing to share' and 'not having to work with girls'. Each group, in turn, was to cover a two-week programme to include two morning sessions at Langleywood. From the beginning, time was at a premium and the time taken to collect and return the pupils by minibus was frustrating. This was further aggravated by what was seen by the Secondary staff as poor punctuality. Throughout the project the relaxed attitude towards timing and the absence of a school bell in the Junior School, so much an integral part of the Secondary system, caused difficulties for the member of staff working between the sites.

The scheme was grounded on the pupils' common sense

notions of energy 'degradation'[5] and the concepts of 'heat' and 'heat flow' were first approached through discussion of tactile experiences and the use of a home survey. A foundation was thus laid for the future treatment of 'energy conservation'.

Langleywood's suite of BBC computers were used to study the heat losses of the pupils own homes. Every effort was made to develop in the pupils a self-consciousness of the methodology employed, the aim being to create in the classroom a genuine collaborative research community anxious to improve society. Whenever possible the pupils were encouraged to measure what they could. We were unable to measure energy because we 'didn't know quite what it was', so we measured the height, the volume of water, the voltage, etc. We looked for clues and patterns from which theories might develop. Small groups chose their own 'energy investigations'. Foxborough's CDT resources were stretched to the full as the programme included opportunities for pupils to make models of 'things that store energy for socially useful purposes' and 'alternative energy supplies'.

At all stages every opportunity was taken to elaborate upon other 'appropriate' technologies. For instance, experiments were conducted to study the heat lost by a 'garah', an unglazed earthenware water cooler. An attempt was made to make connections between concepts of sound energy, technology and the basic properties of musical sound. This was greatly facilitated by the size of the groups and use of the Secondary School resources. The scheme concluded with a consideration of 'world energy demand' predictions, 'energy and our standard of living' and 'social interests and energy policies'.

The all-girl group was first to embark on the two-week rolling programme. They all worked hard, made positive contributions and devised some interesting solutions to the problems identified. One girl used elastic bands and a dynamo to make a model of a machine that could 'store energy for a useful social purpose'. The self-esteem gained by this group as a result of its being the first to embark and thereby able to advise the others was significant. On completing the project, several girls said that although they had enjoyed the project, they had reservations about the usefulness of the work covered. In particular they could not perceive any benefits which might be gained from studying science. They also said that they would have preferred their own class teacher (a woman) to have worked with them on the project instead of the predominantly male staff.

The second group, all boys, constructed several interesting, socially useful models, including a washing machine and a water wheel. A new arrival from Pakistan in the group provided an opportunity to try some of the ILEA Multilingual Science templates.[6] His presence also caused a teacher peripheral to the project to intervene during a practical session with the suggestion that he should not converse in his mother tongue with another Urdu speaker in the group as 'he must learn English'. Language and self-identity are so closely related as to be synonymous in this context and it was necessary to convince this colleague of the importance of concept formation to second language development and of the benefits of multilingualism. On another occasion a peripetetic ESL teacher, holding an illustration of various forms of irrigation technology, made the comment that the boy had 'contributed as much as anyone' to the activity . . . 'because they have these things in Pakistan don't they!' Clearly she had a very rural and patronizing image of the child's formative environment. Such experiences deepened our resolve to effect change.

The mixed group fared less well. After the first week the minibus was damaged and put off the road and as a result much of the programme had to be modified. The work that was produced was, however, encouraging and clearly demonstrated the benefit of using a problem-solving approach. It was interesting to note that, while all these pupils had chosen to opt for a mixed group, they continuously chose to work with one or two friends of the same gender.

A role-play exercise in the final session proved especially interesting with all the groups. Following a discussion of world energy demand and supply trends the pupils were invited to take part in a role play. The role of one of the groups was living in a poor country which had a lot of natural resources. They had to walk for up to six hours a day just to collect twigs for burning. Another group took on the role of old age pensioners in Britain, who found it hard to pay their energy bills. A group chose to represent the group of people who wanted fast cars that use a lot of petrol and another group ran a firm that used large amounts of energy but did not want to spend money to 'Save It' with insulation. Another group pretended to live in East Asia and wanted to build factories to make washing machines and other things that would improve their standard of living. Others lived in a country that still had a lot of oil, although they did not have many factories and did not need to heat their homes. The pupils were given an information sheet summarizing some of the areas covered by the project and were invited to prepare an argument on behalf of their interest group. The ensuing discussion was excellent. The groups were finally instructed to compromise and come up with some policies acceptable to the majority. In every case the pupils chose price increases combined with state help for those in need. They all emphasized the need for everyone to save energy and two of the three groups even suggested that redistributive trade agreements were needed.

## Conclusions

### Role models

The influence of the gender of classteachers in primary schools is likely to be more significant than in secondary if only because she/he is 'our teacher' all of the time. The relationship between the primary school teacher and her/his pupils is closer and children of the same gender are thus likely to identify with them to a greater degree. They have a permanent role model rather than a series of temporary ones. All three groups enjoyed the novelty of working with new members of staff, but many would have preferred a familiar face. The comments of the girls suggest that there is a real need for more positive role models if they are to be encouraged in the science/technology area. In retrospect, more efforts could have been made to identify and invite in women who are working in industry to demonstrate applications. It was difficult to find women working at an appropriate level, however, and this points to the need for the development of some sort of register of visiting speakers. The involvement of a woman secondary science teacher would certainly have been more influential in the project.

### Curriculum

Girls have typically been offered the choice between femininity and equality and it is altogether unsurprising that they have chosen the former. Too often science has been presented as a subject about 'things' rather than about 'people'. We are sure that if we are to develop an anti-sexist and anti-racist science education we must change this. Our focus upon social uses and applications certainly seemed to motivate both the girls and the boys and, significantly, to provide a common ground for discussion in the mixed group.

## Evaluation

In an attempt to assess the effectiveness of the scheme on the pupils an attitude survey was developed using Repertory Grid techniques (Fransella and Bannister, 1984). Unfortunately, it proved impossible in the time to produce a rigorous measure of the project's effectiveness. A great deal was, however, learnt in the attempt. Before the programme began, a series of cards was prepared showing people doing various jobs. The series included black and white people, men and women in a variety of occupations in the rich and poor world. Some were shown in stereotypical roles and others in atypical situations. Each group of pupils was invited to take the cards, presented face down on a table in groups of three and to identify 'something that two had in common but left the other out'. In this way we hoped to identify the pupils' basic constructs of gender, race and employment. It was intended that each of the cards should then be evaluated according to each of these constructs. Unfortunately, in too many cases it seemed that the pupils were addressing their attentions to the specific cards provided rather than the generality as requested. This stage of the exercise thus told us more about the pupils' levels of observation than about their attitudes. What the exercise did provide, however, was the criteria used by the pupils to assess the range of jobs presented. The results showed that gender was the first and most important criterion used. Out of a total of 33 categories of response, the pupils' other significant constructions, in order of inclusion, were 'outdoor/indoor work'; 'high/low in technology'; 'youth'; 'involving children'; 'requiring strength'; 'involving danger'; 'race' and; 'involving machinery'. It was unsurprising but clear that 'involving children' was associated with women and that 'requiring strength' and 'involving danger' was associated with men. Although this is an unremarkable observation in itself, the survey did show just how significant these constructions are to children.

Having failed to develop the instrument in time to assess our project we chose to present the pupils at the end of the scheme with their constructs in polar form as a semantic differential. Discussions suggested that the constructions on high/low in technology and with/without machinery were more complicated and in an effort to clarify the distinctions being made further pupil sub-classifications were used: complicated/simple and advanced/primitive. We invited the pupils to rank each of the jobs this time without seeing the cards.

Again it was unclear that the pupils assessment of jobs always represented their attitudes in any meaningful way, they might still have often been drawing upon uncritical observations of present reality. Table 11.1 shows some of the more interesting aggregated components of the boys' and girls' responses. It seems clear that it is the attitudes of boys that we must counter and the more understanding we have of the development of gender attitudes the more likely we are to be successful. This research suggests that in curriculum terms, we *may* be going in the right direction; it also, incidentally, shows that there is a need for the instruction of boys in child care.

*Epilogue*

As Cottrell (1982) argued in his ASE Nuffield Lecture the twenty-first century is likely to be a 'hungry century'. The world will be hungry for food, raw materials and for energy. In fact, the supply of energy may be the greatest scientific and technological problem of the twenty-first century world. A serious failure to meet the coming needs could lead to the internal collapse of societies, due to civil unrest caused by poverty, unemployment and lost standards of living; or it could lead to global war as countries compete violently for larger shares of inadequate world energy resources. Our pupils must be prepared with an energy education for participating citizenship. This need not dominate the curriculum – experts will certainly be needed, but not everyone needs this expert knowledge. What is essential is that pupils learn that such technologies, just like areas of literature or any other form of knowledge, are at least potentially accessible. They need to develop a critical awareness of the limitations of specialized 'expert' knowledge, and of the issues involved. As the division of labour has developed, so, progressively, the public have been excluded from the control of technology, women and black people have been even further excluded from high-status forms of technological work. Our greatest efforts are therefore needed in redressing this imbalance. We hope that the practical approach to science and technology that we are developing will go some way towards breaking down the alienation experienced

*Table 11.1*  Pupils' assessment of jobs

|  | Feminine (1) (10) Masculine | High in technology (1) (10) Low in technology | Safe (1) (10) Dangerous | Requires strength (1) (10) No strength needed | Black people (1) (10) White people | Dirty job (1) (10) Clean job | Complicated (1) (10) Simple | Advanced (1) (10) Primitive |
|---|---|---|---|---|---|---|---|---|
| *Boys' responses* | | | | | | | | |
| Driving | 5 | 4 | 8 | 5 | 5 | 6 | 4 | 5 |
| Child care | 4 | 6 | 3 | 6 | 5 | 10 | 6 | 8 |
| Civil eng. | 9 | 2 | 7 | 4 | 5 | 4 | 3 | 4 |
| Office work | 4 | 4 | 3 | 7 | 5 | 8 | 4 | 4 |
| Electronics | 6 | 2 | 9 | 5 | 5 | 7 | 3 | 3 |
| Mining | 9 | 5 | 9 | 4 | 5 | 2 | 5 | 6 |
| Science | 6 | 2 | 7 | 5 | 5 | 6 | 2 | 2 |
| Teaching | 6 | 4 | 3 | 5 | 5 | 8 | 4 | 4 |
| *Girls' responses* | | | | | | | | |
| Driving | 5 | 4 | 6 | 7 | 5 | 6 | 5 | 4 |
| Child care | 3 | 7 | 5 | 6 | 5 | 6 | 4 | 5 |
| Civil eng. | 7 | 3 | 7 | 3 | 5 | 3 | 3 | 4 |
| Office work | 4 | 3 | 3 | 8 | 5 | 8 | 5 | 4 |
| Electronics | 6 | 3 | 6 | 7 | 5 | 6 | 3 | 3 |
| Mining | 9 | 6 | 7 | 3 | 5 | 2 | 4 | 4 |
| Science | 5 | 4 | 5 | 7 | 5 | 5 | 3 | 3 |
| Teaching | 5 | 5 | 3 | 7 | 5 | 7 | 4 | 4 |

by many pupils and that science may be seen at last as a subject to be grasped to achieve practical ends, to solve real problems and transform aspects of our society for the common good.

## Notes

1 A more detailed analysis is presented, along with information/ activity sheets, attitude survey materials and data produced as part of the project in 'The Langleywood/Foxborough Energy Project Pack', available from Slough Teachers' Centre, Thomas Gray Centre, Queens Road, Slough.

2 This report is significant in defining the educational under-achievement of black children in terms of racism in education and the wider society. As its title, *Education for All*, suggests, the report seeks to promote changes in the education of all children to dismantle such racism.

3 'Secondary Students' Ideas about Energy', workshop pack, Children's Learning in Science Project, CSSME, The University of Leeds, Leeds, LS2 9JT.

4 The Association for Curriculum Development in Science, Henry Smith, Holland Park School, Airlie Gardens, London W8 7AF.

5 The arguments against grounding such schemes in the more popular ideas of 'conservation', are usefully outlined in Driver and Millar (1985). The following view is considered typical: 'That Principle of Conservation of Energy, Miss, I don't believe it. You know, when you have a battery and a lamp, and the battery has electrical energy right? And it goes to heat and light in the lamp. Well, I mean, the heat evaporates and the light goes dim. So the energy has gone. It isn't there is it?' (Black and Solomon, 1983).

6 Available from the North London Science Teachers' Centre, 62–66 Highbury Grove, London N5 2AD.

## Recommended reading

J. Craig and D.G. Ayres (1988) 'Does Primary Science Affect Girls' and Boys' Interest in Science?'. *School Science Review*, vol. 69, no. 128.

Dawn Gill and Les Levidow (eds) (1987) *Anti-Racist Science Teaching*, Free Association Books.

A. Kelly (ed.) (1981) *The Missing Half: Girls and Science Education*, Manchester Univ. Press 1981.

S. Toulmin (1982) 'The Construal of Reality: Criticism in Modern and Postmodern Science', *Critical Inquiry*, 9 September.

R. Driver (1983) *The Pupil as Scientist?*, Open University Press.

# References

Amos, Valerie and Parmar, Pratibha (1984) 'Challenging Imperial Feminism', *Feminist Review*, no. 17.

APU (1986) *Girls and Physics*, APU Occasional Paper no. 4, DES.

Askew, Sue and Ross, Carol (1988) *Boys Don't Cry*, Open University Press.

Askew, Sue and Ross, Carol (1985) *Anti-Sexist Work with Boys*, ILEA.

Barnes, Douglas (1969) *Language, the Learner, and the School*, Penguin.

Belotti, Elena (1975) *Little Girls*, Writers and Readers.

Black, P. and Solomon, J. (1983) 'Life-world and science world – pupil ideas about energy', *Entropy in the school*, vol. 1. Roland Eotvos Physical Society, Budapest, Hungary.

Bradford (1986). *Gender Issues Training for Teachers and Lecturers*. Directorate of Educational Services, Bradford Metropolitan Council, Provincial House, Bradford BD1 1NP.

Brent (1985a) *Steps to Equality*, Handbook for Primary Teachers, Brent LEA, CDSU, Donnington Road, Willsden, London NW10.

Brent (1985b) *Working Now*, Brent LEA, CDSU, Donnington Road, Willsden, London NW10.

Brent (1986) *Design it, Build it, Use it*, Brent LEA, CDSU, Donnington Road, Willsden, London NW10.

Cottrell, Alan (1982) 'Science after the year 2000', *School Science Review*, vol. 62, September, p. 15.

Department of Education and Science (1985). *Education for All*. HMSO (Swann Report).

Donaldson, Margaret (1978) *Children's Minds*, Fontana.

Driver, Rosalind and Millar, Robin (eds) (1986) *Energy Matters*, University of Leeds.

EOC (nd (a)) *An Equal Start*.

EOC (nd (b)) *Equal Opportunities and the School Governor*.

EOC (1980) *Promotion and the Woman Teacher*.

EOC (1985) *Equal Opportunities and the Woman Teacher.*

Fransella, Fay and Bannister, Don (1984) *A Manual for Repertory Grid Technique*, Academic Press.

Gadsby, D. and Hoggarth, J. (1980) *Alleluya: 77 Songs for thinking people*, A. & C. Black.

Martin Grant (1984) *Presenting Design and Technology to Girls*, Girls and Technology (GATE) Report, 84, 2, Centre for Science and Maths. Education, Chelsea College, Bridges Place, London SW6.

Holland, Janet (1987) 'Girls and Occupational Choice Project', Working Paper no. 10, Dept of Sociology, Institute of Education, London University.

Harrop, Beatrice (ed.) (1976) *Okki-Tokki-Unga: Action Songs for Children*, A. & C. Black.

ILEA (1983) *Race, Sex and Class.*

ILEA (1986) *Primary Matters.*

Kemp, Gene (1979) *The Turbulent Term of Tyke Tiler*, Penguin.

Langer, Suzanne (1953) *Feeling and Form*, RKP.

Lees, Sue (1986) 'Sex, Race and Culture: Feminism and the Limits of Cultural Pluralism', *Feminist Review*, 22.

MacDonald, Madeleine (1980) 'Schooling and the Reproduction of Class and Gender Relations' in L. Barton and P. Maughan (eds), *Schooling, Ideology and the Curriculum*, Falmer Press.

Maidenhead Teachers' Centre (1983) *Doing Things.*

Matterson, Elizabeth M. (ed.) (1969) *This Little Puffin: Finger Plays and nursery games*, Penguin.

Miller, Jane (1983) *Many voices: bilingualism, culture and education*, RKP.

Munsch, Robert N. (1982) *The Paper Bag Princess*, Hippo Books, Scholastic Publications.

Myers, Kate (ed.) (1987) *Genderwatch 1: Self-Assessment Schedules for Use in Schools*, SCDC Publications.

NUT (1987) *Teacher 3: Equality.*

NUT (1988) *Towards Equality for Girls and Boys: Guidelines on Countering Sexism in Schools.*

O'Neill, Cecily and Lambert, Alan (1982) *Drama Structures*, Hutchinson.

Smith, Frank (1986) *Collaboration in the Classroom*, Reading and Language Information Centre in conjunction with Abel Press, Victoria, BC.

Spender, Dale (1984) *Time and Tide Wait for No Man*, Pandora.

Spender, Dale (1982) *Invisible Women . . . The Schooling Scandal*, Writers and Readers.

Spender, Dale (1980) *Man-Made Language*, RKP.

Taylor, Hazel (1985) 'A Local Authority Initiative on Equal Opportunities' in M. Arnot (ed.), *Race and Gender: Equal*

*Opportunities Policies in Education*, Pergamon Press.

Walkerdine, Valerie (1981) 'Sex, Power and Pedagogy', *Screen Education*, 38.

Walkerdine, Valerie (1984) 'Some Day My Prince Will Come' in Angela McRobbie and Mica Nava (ed.), *Gender and Generation*, Macmillan.

Wallis, M. (1987) *Job Hunting for Women*, Kogan Page.

West Kent NUT (1985) *Unequal Opportunities and West Kent Teachers*.

Weiner, Gaby (1986) 'Feminist Education and Equal Opportunities: Unity or discord?', *British Journal of Sociology of Education*, 7, 3.

Whyte, Judith (1983) *Beyond the Wendy House: Sex Role Stereotyping in Primary Schools*, Longman (for SCDC).

Willes, Mary (1981) 'Children Becoming Pupils: A Study of Discourse in Nursery and Reception Classes' in Clem Adelman (ed.), *Uttering, Muttering*, Grant McIntyre.

Wright, Cecile (1987) 'The Relation between Teachers and Afro-Caribbean Pupils: Observing Multi-racial Classrooms' in G. Weiner and M. Arnot (eds), *Gender under Scrutiny*, Hutchinson.

# Index

Amos, Valerie, 2
APU *see* Assessment of
Performance Unit
assessment, 39
Assessment of Performance Unit,
101
Association for Curriculum
Development in Science, 101,
109

Bannister, Don, 106
Barnes, Douglas, 9
Beat, Kim, 95
Belotti, Elena, 83
bilingualism, 4, 52–61, 62–70, 104
boys
aggression/violence, 29, 31, 34,
35, 71–9, 81
behaviour problems, 81, 93
CDT, 46, 49, 50
identity/role, 12, 13, 101
language, 11, 68
power, 11, 13, 33
self-segregation, 24, 81, 102
stereotypes, 26, 27, 37, 38, 39,
46, 53, 56, 80, 83, 85, 95, 107
Brent (Local Education
Authority), 1, 46, 47, 79, 93
Britton, James, 9
Brooker, Nicola, ix, 4, 71–9

Campbell, Annie, ix, 4, 71–9
careers, 7, 14–20, 25, 26
CDT, *see* Craft, Design and
Technology
Childrens Learning in Science
Project, 101, 109

construction kits, 12, 46–51
Cottrell, Alan, 107
Craft, Design and Technology, 3,
37–45, 46–51, 83, 95, 102
curriculum, 37, 47, 50, 93, 94,
98, 100, 101, 107, 109
hidden curriculum, 57, 73
*see also* National Curriculum

D'Arcy, Sue, ix, 4, 80–91
Department of Education and
Science, 101
*Design It, Build It, Use It!* (Brent
1986), 47
disability, 86
Donaldson, Margaret, 9
drama, 3, 23–36, 60
Driver, R., 109

Education Act (1944), 65
*Education for All see* Swann
Report
Egan, Bridget, ix, 3, 37–45
EOC *see* Equal Opportunities
Commission
equal opportunities, 7, 8, 14–20,
55, 92–9, 100
Equal Opportunities Commission,
14, 15, 16, 17

Forsyth, Liz, ix, 4, 62–70
Fransella, Fay, 106

Gadsby, D., 90
gender roles, 23, 25, 27, 39
in fiction, 55

'Genderwatch', 11
girls
    bilingualism, 57, 59, 68
    CDT, 12, 37–45, 46, 48, 49, 50,
        83
    science, 101–9
    self-segregation, 24, 27
    sexism, 52–61, 76, 80
    stereotypes, 7, 26, 33, 37, 53,
        55, 78, 80, 95

Hoggarth, J., 90
Holland, Janet, 7
humour, 9, 74
Hunt, Roderick, 88

ILEA *see* Inner London Education
    Authority
'Individualized Approach to
    Reading', 88
Inner London Education
    Authority, 1, 10, 79, 101

Kahn, Peter, 14

Lambert, Alan, 30
Langer, Suzanne, 3
Langleywood/Foxborough Energy
    Project (Slough), 109
language, 4, 11, 62–70, 96, 104
Lees, Sue, 2
Loud, Jeremy, ix, 4, 100–10

Macdonald, Madeleine, 1
Matterson, Elizabeth M., 89
Micro Electronic Support Unit, 45
Millar, R., 109
Moon, Cliff, 88
multicultural education, 8, 23, 52,
    53–61, 62–70, 93, 94
Myers, Kate, 11

National Advisory Committee for
    Equal Opportunities, 19
National Curriculum, 2, 23
National Union of Teachers, 15–19
NUT *see* National Union of
    Teachers

O'Neill, Cecily, 30
'Oxford Reading Tree', 88

Parmar, Pratibha, 2

racial equality, 53, 62–70, 93, 94,
    100, 101
reading schemes, 88, 94
role models, 14, 19, 101, 105

*Scene* (BBC), 96
Seacole, Mary, 77
science, 4, 83, 100–9
sexism, 2, 7, 8, 52–61, 71–9, 80,
    100, 101
Shamaris, Christina, x, 3, 52–61
Sherwin, Jo, x, 3, 46–51
Siraj-Blatchford, John, x, 4,
    100–10
Slough Industrial Language
    Centre, 63
Smith, Frank, 2, 4
Spender, Dale, 1, 84, 92
stereotyping, 7, 26, 27, 28, 33, 37,
    39, 46, 48, 53, 55, 58, 78,
    80–3, 85, 87, 88, 95, 106
Swann Report (DES), 101, 109

Taylor, Hazel, 8, 95
Taylor, Margaret, 52, 54, 60
*Times Educational Supplement*, 8
*Towards Equality for Girls and
    Boys* (NUT 1989), 19
*Turbulent Term of Tyke Tyler,
    The* (Kemp), 25
Tutchell, Derek, x, 4, 92–9
Tutchell, Eva, x, 1–4, 7–13, 55, 56

Vick, Helen, x, 3, 23–36

Walkerdine, Valerie, 11, 27, 60
Wallis, M., 17
Weiner, Gaby, 4
Whyte, Judith, 43
Willes, Mary, 11
Wootton Freeman, Sue, xi, 3,
    14–20
work (in school), 39, 40–5
Wright, Cecile, 84